SEVEN QUESTIONS ABOUT LIFE AND FAITH

WHAT GEN Z
REALLY
WANTS TO
KNOW ABOUT
GOD

TANITA TUALLA MADDOX

FOREWORD BY CHAP CLARK

ivp

An imprint of InterVarsity Press
Downers Grove, Illinois

I0202082

InterVarsity Press
P.O. Box 1400 | Downers Grove, IL 60515-1426
ivpress.com | email@ivpress.com

©2025 by Tanita Tualla Maddox

All rights reserved. No part of this book may be reproduced in any form without written permission from InterVarsity Press.

InterVarsity Press® is the publishing division of InterVarsity Christian Fellowship/USA®. For more information, visit intervarsity.org.

All Scripture quotations, unless otherwise indicated, are taken from The Holy Bible, New International Version®, NIV®. Copyright © 1973, 1978, 1984, 2011 by Biblica, Inc.™ Used by permission of Zondervan. All rights reserved worldwide. www.zondervan.com. The "NIV" and "New International Version" are trademarks registered in the United States Patent and Trademark Office by Biblica, Inc.™

While any stories in this book are true, some names and identifying information may have been changed to protect the privacy of individuals.

The publisher cannot verify the accuracy or functionality of website URLs used in this book beyond the date of publication.

Cover design: Faceout Studio, Jeff Miller
Interior design: Daniel van Loon
Images: © Masahiro Makino / Moment via Getty Images

ISBN 978-1-5140-1216-1 (print) | ISBN 978-1-5140-1217-8 (digital)

Printed in the United States of America ⊗

Library of Congress Cataloging-in-Publication Data
A catalog record for this book is available from the Library of Congress.

31   30   29   28   27   26   25 | 13   12   11   10   9   8   7   6   5   4   3   2   1

"By breaking down the burning questions Gen Z is asking, Tanita Tualla Maddox gives us a window to better understand the next generation while also providing a lens to see Scripture with fresh eyes. You'll see Gen Z in a new, compassionate light and grasp how the gospel speaks directly to every generation. Winsome, well-researched, and practical, this is a book for anyone who's working with Gen Z, cares about a Gen Zer, knows a Gen Zer, or all of the above."

Newt Crenshaw, president and CEO of Young Life

"If you are a parent of a Gen Zer or you work with this amazing generation, you will want to read this book. Not only is it well written and informative, but the research is amazing. Tanita Tualla Maddox gets it when it comes to Gen Z, and she lives it out in her life work. Her insight, wisdom, and passion are evident on every page. She understands the mind, heart, soul, and needs of Gen Zers like few I know."

Jim Burns, founder of HomeWord and author of *Doing Life with Your Adult Children*

"I have been familiar with Tanita Tualla Maddox's academic work for several years. I am very encouraged to see that it is now more broadly available. It will generate many ideas among those who desire to understand and minister to Gen Z."

David R. Dunaetz, professor of leadership and organizational psychology at Azusa Pacific University and editor of the *Great Commission Research Journal*

"Young people are tired of us answering questions they're not asking. If you're an adult who'd like to understand young people's real questions, how they are unique for this generation, and how Jesus intersects with the answers, then this book is for you. You'll gain deep principles and everyday practices to have better conversations and connections with the young people you care about most."

Kara Powell, chief of leadership formation at Fuller Seminary and coauthor of *Future-Focused Church*

"Aiming to understand rather than fix Gen Zers, Tanita Tualla Maddox's book offers hope for pastors, parents, and mentors. Each chapter delivers valuable insights to engage with Gen Z's experiences for the sake of the gospel. *What Gen Z Really Wants to Know About God* centers around seven questions that will transform your perspective of Gen Z and enhance your ability to connect across generations. Because every generation faces challenges in understanding the next, Maddox's book is an essential resource for those who disciple the upcoming generation."

Sharon R. Hoover, author of *Mapping Church Missions*

"Getting to know each new generation and learning how to love them well can be confusing and tiring. That's why I so appreciate generational guides like Tanita Tualla Maddox. Her new book *What Gen Z Really Wants to Know About God* offers the clarity and encouragement I need to press on as an itinerant minister who's committed to getting to know and love every wonderful new generation that comes along."

Don Everts, author of *I Once Was Lost*

"As Gen Z students enter the spaces where we work and serve, many of us feel uncertain about how to connect with this generation in ways that are meaningful and relevant. *What Gen Z Really Wants to Know About God* steps into this confusion and provides a clear path forward. Through an insightful exploration of Gen Z's values and burning questions, Tanita Tualla Maddox creatively ties these concerns to a contextualized presentation of the gospel, challenging our paradigms while equipping us to engage in fresh ways. By applying Maddox's wisdom—gained from years of working with young adults—we can open doors to discipleship for a generation eager to discover their place in the biblical story."

Erica Young Reitz, founder of After College Transition and author of *After College*

"Tanita Tualla Maddox provides a firsthand perspective and keen insight into the hearts and minds of Gen Z and how to meaningfully connect with and understand them. She skillfully illuminates the questions, struggles, and culture of the generation while outlining practical wisdom on how to contextualize the gospel to their real life. She displays a deep love and admiration for the meaningful impact Gen Z can bring to the church and the world. If you want to better reach and disciple Gen Z—which should be every believer—this is a must-read."

Randy Templeton and Ashley Cope, cofounders of Darkroom Faith

"This is a breath of fresh air. A timely resource connecting those serving in ministry to the questions and, more importantly, to the reasons behind the questions that Gen Z is asking about God."

Elliot Wnek, campus director for Athletes in Action in Southern Arizona

"If you are a pastor, parent, teacher, leader, or friend of anyone that is Gen Z, I urge you to *run* and read this book. With clarity and compassion, Tanita Tualla Maddox teaches through accessible stories, data, and scriptural reasoning how to listen, speak, and understand differently in order to love, serve, and empower the complex, beautiful, and hurting generation that is Gen Z. Read and get schooled in the best way to love the next generation and beyond."

Sarah Shin, lecturer at Westminster Theological Centre and author of *Beyond Colorblind*

DEDICATED TO MY HUSBAND,

W. ASHLEY,

who started me on this journey,

a gifted filmmaker and storyteller

who encouraged me to tell

the story of a generation.

CONTENTS

FOREWORD

CHAP CLARK

Let the little children come to me, and do not hinder
them, for the kingdom of God belongs to such as these.

JESUS (MARK 10:14)

For decades the "adult" world has had a hard time with emerging generations. Gen X and Millennials were a problem to be analyzed, labeled, and fixed. The questions for us were, "How do we get young people to care about the church?" and "Who can we hire to bring them back?" In our discipleship efforts, all too often what we were really saying was, "How do we make them become, well, *us*?" In so doing we both missed them and failed them.

Along comes Gen Z. The chasm is wider today, for lots of reasons. Many decry that "we are losing our kids," looking to statistics and anecdotes that overwhelmingly reinforce that when it comes to faith and the church, young people are running for the door. We see Gen Z as leaving us. But what if we are the ones who turned our backs on them? This is a generation who longs for connection, inclusion, and truth, yet we still blame them for the disconnect. Instead of welcoming the young and embracing who they are, we may actually be *hindering* them from coming to Jesus.

If you care about and want to know how to rethink the church's response to Gen Z, then you have a friend in Tanita Maddox. When she allowed herself to ask, "Am I out of touch with this new generation?" she realized it was not the responsibility of "Gen Zers" to initiate a bridge to us, so she went to them. As she did, Tanita discovered that Gen Z has much to teach us.

In *What Gen Z Really Wants to Know About God*, Tanita provides a well-researched, accessible, and personal resource for understanding the mind and heart of Gen Z. Each chapter is a puzzle piece. Begin with the question that is most pressing to you. Move on to an issue that might make little sense to you. Take what you read and share it with others. Then go into the field and observe and listen to teenagers and emerging adults. As you allow this puzzle to come together, you will find yourself entering a whole new world of what biblical community is all about. For God's people to build a bridge to Gen Z is not unlike connecting to any outsider. We have much to offer, but, even more importantly, we have much to learn. For to see Gen Z as talented, insightful, dedicated, and committed to knowing and following truth is to be the church that Jesus commissioned and called us to be.

WHAT'S GOING ON WITH GEN Z AND THE CHURCH?

Have I become irrelevant?

There has probably been a moment in the last few years when we looked at the ministry we were doing and asked: *Am I effective anymore?* For me, that moment arrived when Generation Z (Gen Z) entered the doors of the building. There was a shift I couldn't put my finger on, but I knew something had changed. I saw panic attacks at events, students with too much anxiety to go to school, girls who would only meet with me one-on-one and not in groups, open hostility to faith unlike what I had seen before, and more. I hadn't changed what I was doing, but I was experiencing a very different outcome. I had been leading youth ministry for twenty years, but was suddenly feeling lost, like I had no idea what I was doing. *Why is what has worked for so long no longer working?* My first inclination was to think there was something wrong with me; I was the problem. I had gotten too old for this, and I wasn't effective in ministry anymore. *Have I become irrelevant?*

After a little digging, I realized there had been a generational shift, and Gen Z had arrived so quickly, we didn't realize they were here until the oldest members of the generation were graduating from high school. Gen Z wasn't the problem though. The problem was a disconnect between me, the way I had always done things, and this new generation. I did not know or understand Gen Z.

I realized I was out of touch, and I had better figure out who they are, what they are looking for, and what they are asking, in order to better share the gospel with them and help them grow in their faith, or risk becoming increasingly ineffective and irrelevant.[1] So I began to listen, study, and read. I spent days, weeks, months, and now years seeking to understand the next generation. This book is an extension of my doctoral thesis.[2] I became committed to knowing Gen Z, both in study and relationship, so I could better share the gospel and disciple this generation.

GEN Z FLIGHT

There has been a lot of buzz around younger generations leaving the church, and a lot of speculation about why. Gen Z is more likely than previous generations to be raised by parents who have no religious affiliation (those who would check the box *atheist*, *agnostic*, or *none*).[3] Even those Gen Zers who were practicing Christians when they were younger are leaving churches. As Gen Z ages into their twenties, a significant portion turn away from Christianity or Christian communities like churches.[4] A 2023 survey by Springtide Research Center found four-in-ten Gen Zers (aged 13–25) never attend religious services.[5] The Survey Center on American Life also found Gen Z is leaving their faith at younger ages than previous generations, with 48 percent of those leaving doing so between ages 13 and 17, and 26 percent of those leaving doing so between ages 18 and 29.[6]

Looking at surveys regarding Gen Z and the Christian faith, it's hard to decipher what version of Christian faith they are leaving. According to the Jesus Survey, most Gen Z Christians agree Jesus, Mohammed, Buddha, and other belief systems or religions all have equal value and standing when it comes to the afterlife.[7] This survey was conducted in 2012, just as Gen Z were becoming teenagers, and exhibits the influences on Gen Z as they grew up. These are Christians—those who have professed faith in Jesus Christ—who also believe all roads lead to heaven. This does not translate into religious practice for Gen Z, such as attending church services or reading the Bible. As of 2023, 68 percent of Gen Z agree there are many religions they agree with.[8]

According to sources such as the American Bible Society and others, Gen Z is also not familiar with the Bible or the stories of the Bible, or how to read or understand the Bible.[9] I recently sat with a college student who was brought up in a Christian family, was active in her faith, and had attended church her whole life. I was referring to the stories of Joseph and Moses as she was wrestling with having a multiethnic background, and thus shared a multicultural experience with these Old Testament heroes. She was unfamiliar with these stories, and I had to do an overview summary to get her caught up. The felt-board Bible stories from my childhood Sunday school classes were unfamiliar to my Gen Z friend. I've also sat with a recent high school graduate who in the midst of our conversation said, "But Jesus sinned too, right?" These are not outlier kinds of conversations. They are the conversations with a generation, even the Christians in that generation, who do not know what is in the Bible. With the absence of knowledge, Gen Z is making guesses, and it ripples out into not knowing what to believe about the Bible.

There are concerns and questions around Gen Z and the future of Christianity. What if Gen Z isn't just leaving, but they weren't here to begin with? In 2023, 31 percent of Gen Zers said they had never participated in a religious or spiritual community.[10] Many such as Pew Research note it's not just Gen Z's interest or belief in Christianity that has decreased, but belief in all religions.[11] Overall, Gen Z is not engaging with faith. As Gen Z is moving from middle schools and high schools to college campuses and careers, the impact on churches and ministries is more widely felt. Seeing the decline of engagement by the next generation, many churches and ministries are looking for answers to questions like:

- Why is Gen Z leaving the Christian faith?
- How do we reach Gen Z with the gospel?
- What does discipling Gen Z look like?
- What is going on with Gen Z and the church?

These are good and important questions to ask. A positive dynamic that has come with the arrival of Gen Z is that churches and ministries have done some self-examination to figure out where the disconnect is.

A Barna Group study highlighted one such disconnect between Gen Z and older Christian adults: the faith and gospel prioritized by churches are not the same faith and gospel prioritized by Gen Z.[12] This isn't to say that there is more than one faith and one gospel, but in the full breadth and depth of the Christian faith and gospel, both parties are focused on different aspects. According to *Church Doesn't End with Z,*

Gen Z does not see a connection between the gospel they are hearing at church and their everyday lives; the gospel seems irrelevant.[13] Churches are not addressing the questions around faith and meaning that matter to the next generation.[14] What is being communicated to Gen Z is "that God is not concerned about the world they inhabit—and presumably that God is not concerned about them."[15]

GENERATIONAL DISCONNECT

About twelve years ago, I took a course with David Livermore, author of *Cultural Intelligence,* and an example he used stuck with me. He asked the class this question: "Why did the prodigal son go hungry?" (see Luke 15:11-20). I was quick to answer, "Because he squandered all of his money." But the story points to three big reasons why the prodigal son was hungry: (1) there was a famine, (2) no one would give him anything to eat, and (3) he spent all his money. Livermore pointed out that depending on our cultural context, we all may answer that question differently.

For the sake of this example, let's say older Christian adults cite the reason for the prodigal son's situation is (3) he spent all his money, but Gen Zers agree that (2) no one would give him anything to eat. Gen Z is focused on community and charity, while older Christians are focused on personal stewardship and responsibility. They are looking at the same passage, but not having the same conversation. They are prioritizing and focusing on different things, both valuable parts of the passage. This is what is meant by Gen Z and the older generations of Christians (who are leading our churches and ministries) not prioritizing the same faith or same gospel. As a result, the church and Gen Z aren't having the same conversation and are missing each other. No one is at any fault, but we need to learn how to get back into the same conversation.

Gen Z has the perception that the church is not open to, or is even hostile to, doubts and skepticism. The evangelism and discipleship that many of us practice do not fully address Gen Z's life experiences, and many Gen Zers feel they cannot talk about it. For Gen Z, this translates to a lack of belonging in the Christian faith. They think, *If you want to belong, accept everything that is taught and don't ask questions or have doubts.* By asking our Gen Zers a question that opens the door to their questions, we can demonstrate that there is room for them and all of their questions, doubts, and skepticism in conversation with Jesus.

Studies from both faith-based and non-faith-based research reveal that Gen Z views Christians and followers of the Christian faith as ignorant, uninformed, hypocritical, irrelevant, and judgmental.[16] This doesn't leave me with a warm and fuzzy feeling inside. It makes me pause to see the lens a generation is looking through as they look at me. This could be a result of churches and ministries continuing the same messages and methods without considering who their audience is (and this is exactly what I was doing). What has worked for previous generations is not working for this one.

It is time for many of us to admit that we don't know or understand Gen Z. The good news is that we want to understand! We want to because we deeply care about and believe in Gen Z.

Hold on a second. Pause and consider this question before continuing: *Do I care about and believe in Gen Z?* Is it possible that we want to care about and believe in Gen Z, but don't currently? Is it that we tolerate Gen Z, but since they aren't going away, we might as well figure out how to coexist with them? A friend once told me the most important part of finding directions on a map isn't necessarily knowing where you are going, but knowing where you are now. Being honest, maybe uncomfortably honest, about where we are as we embark on this journey together is crucial to the process.

Right now, the church is answering questions Gen Z is not asking while ignoring the ones they do ask. This furthers a disconnection between the Christian faith and the realities of everyday life for Gen Z. When many young Gen Zers were asked how much God is relevant to them, they answered, "Not much at all."[17] When we ignore the questions Gen Z is asking, Gen Z doesn't have an opportunity to see how the Bible is relevant to the longings of their hearts and souls. This means the conversation around faith and the gospel does not intersect the worldview or experience of Gen Z in a meaningful way, even though it could! After all, the gospel is good news for everyone, everywhere, throughout time.

The *way* the gospel is presented has been contextualized for the audience from the beginning. The work of contextualization is the work of the church to bring the gospel to all people.[18] Contextualization is the intentional work of cultural translation to help the audience understand the gospel in their own language, in a way that is relevant to their experience. It's the gospel presented through the lens of the audience, not the speaker. Practicing cultural exegesis is strategic for evangelism for Gen Z.[19] We must do the work of contextualizing the gospel for Gen Z and contextualize what it means to be a disciple of Christ. This is not as difficult as it sounds. It has been modeled to us by God in his Word.

Though God exists outside of a specific cultural context, God interacts with us within our cultural context. This is seen throughout the Bible, as God interacts with people within their time, place, family, cultural belief system, and worldview. He acted and spoke in ways that were significant to the audience, using illustrations and metaphors that had specific meaning to those people at that time in that place. He went as far as to enter into the world as a human child.

We cannot be removed from our human and cultural context to enter a divine level to understand God, so God meets us where we are. In that, something amazing happens. God may start with where we are at, but he pulls us closer to him. He accepts us as we are, and at the same time, while God is accepting us, he changes us to be more like him.

CONNECTING WITH GEN Z

Gen Z has its own generational context and culture, which includes the questions this generation is asking based on its members' worldview and values. If churches and ministries understand these questions, the context around these questions, as well as how Christianity reflects the values and questions of Gen Z, a more relevant and applicable faith journey can be presented to Gen Z. They can then understand that Jesus cares about, understands, and engages with their hearts and their real lives in a meaningful and real way.

In this book, we are going to identify questions Gen Z is asking based on their values, experiences, and worldview. The goal is to equip older generations of Christians to provide relevant and meaningful answers to Gen Z's questions with the gospel and discipleship. Let's connect the dots between real life, along with its real questions and doubts, with the Christian faith. We will discuss how to open our Bibles side by side with our Gen Z friends to unpack the Word together in evangelism and discipleship. Why not invite a Gen Zer in your life to read this along with you? Don't take my words for it, take theirs! Circle and underline passages and ideas, point to them and ask, "What do you think?"

If you are a member of Gen Z, this is a time to reflect on your own values, experiences, and worldview, in conjunction with your larger generational context. Examine how the Christian faith provides answers to the questions your generation asks, but also engages Gen Z values and experiences through life as a disciple of Christ. Take the opportunity to invite an older adult Christian to read and discuss alongside you. I hope it opens the door to further conversation, and ultimately you feel seen, known, and valued.[20]

WHO IS GENERATION Z?

"What is great about being a member of Gen Z?"

I asked this question to an upperclassman last year. I like to ask my own children that question for their ages: "What is great about being eight years old?" My son beams and says things like, "It's so great! You get to play outside with your friends, ride bikes, and play hide-and-seek. Someone else does my laundry and makes me yummy food. I get to read in my room before bedtime and snuggle with you!" I share this to provide context, because when I asked the same question to a Gen Zer, I did not get the same response.

"What is great about being Gen Z?"

This upperclassman looked straight into my eyes with a deadpan expression and responded, "Is there anything?"

I noticed two college students next to me at a coffee shop today, so I leaned over and asked them if I could ask them a question. They agreed, so I asked, "What is great about being Gen Z?" Their first response was to look at each other, perplexed, and then they started laughing in their own discomfort with the question. They both needed a moment to come up with a response.

I have to wonder if that response is a surprise. What do you think Gen Z hears about themselves from older generations or the media? Go ahead and pick up your phone and ask some Gen Zers in your life. I have asked hundreds of Gen Zers this question, and the same answers pop up over and over again. How do they hear their generation described? *Weak, fragile, snow-flakes, entitled, self-centered, over-emotional, confused, anxious,* and so on. I have never had any Gen Zer bring up one positive thing they hear. It breaks my heart. In our lack of understanding, let us never refer to Generation Z as fragile. It is an unfair label to a generation of people who are indeed strong, but often strong in ways unseen or unrecognized by older generations.

The next generation will live into the words we speak over them, so we should consider what words we are speaking over Gen Z. We, older generations, are responsible for raising, stew-arding, and discipling the next generation, and right now, they are hearing from us, "We don't like you." I picked up a printed manuscript of this very book at an office supply store, and the employee behind the counter said, "I just saw Gen Z on the cover, and just thinking about Gen Z gives me a headache!"

Now, as Gen Z is entering adulthood, they have started to complain about the generation following them: Gen Alpha. I have heard Gen Zers refer to Gen Alpha as feral badgers and as a doomed generation. In their frustration or annoyance in asking "What is wrong with this Alpha generation?," Gen Z is simply repeating what we have modeled for them: complaining about the next generation.

I think we can model a different way. We can change the message our young people hear from us. We still have time and plenty of opportunity to speak vision, hope, and gratitude for

Gen Z. We can identify the ways Gen Z reflects the image of God, and encourage them in this, because it is different from the ways other generations reflect the image of God. To do so, we need to listen to the Lord, so that we can see our young generation through his eyes.

WHO IS GEN Z?

Gen Z (born 1997–2012[1]) is the largest, most diverse generation in the United States, but Gen Z is also globally connected and makes up almost a third of the global population.[2] Gen Z was the first American generation raised in a culturally post-Christian United States.[3] Gen Z isn't simply leaving the church, but they are carrying into adulthood the impacts of their cultural surroundings.

Generational culture. It is helpful to begin the conversation by recognizing that generations have their own distinct cultures. This means Gen Z has its own generational culture, distinct from previous generations. If older generations feel like there is a communication breakdown, it's because there is one. Gen Z has its own way of communicating and use of language (and I don't mean slang, no cap). We can use the same words, and those words have different meanings to different generations. Terms like *acceptance*, *safe*, *respectful*, and *appropriate* are a few examples of these. Generational cultures have their own cultural values, taboos, mores, and experiences.

Safe. Safety is a top value for Gen Z, who are consistently analyzing: "Is it safe?"[4] Gen Z wants to feel safe all of the time, which involves different types of safety, including physical, emotional, psychological, perceived, and so on. Their value and search for safety prompts Gen Z to actively "mitigate risk and challenges" in their lives.[5] This has led to the belief and practice that if something is not safe, it must be avoided.

Digital connection. Gen Z is often described as digitally native. They have had access to interactive, smart technology for most of their lives and are first-language speakers in the digital space. Gen Zers seem to flow seamlessly between the real world and the digital one, integrating the culture of the digital space into the real world and forming a third, blended culture in which they live. This is not limited to certain demographics of Gen Z. By 2015, race and socioeconomic differences did not have a measurable impact on social media use by Gen Z,[6] wiping out an internet gap that once existed between social classes in the United States, and eventually, around the world. Gen Z is digitally proficient and connected, with constant access to endless information. They are first-language, digital speakers and understand the digital space fluently. This generation has been marked by smartphones and access to interactive, digital technology from a young age and throughout most of their lives.

This access to social and digital media has impacted mental and physical health, identity and worldview formation, and the form and function of relationships. Digital and social media have also constructed a global system for communication, education, and relationships that Gen Z would be disadvantaged to leave behind. The softball team at our local high school communicated important information through Snapchat. One of the players told me she was constantly missing updates on practices or what to wear on game days because her parents did not allow her to have Snapchat. I thought about different youth activities, classes, or churches. How much information is shared in a digital form, and more specifically, through a social media app? Would someone miss out if they were not on social media?

Technology accelerates the pace at which the world is moving. Most of what is happening is shared in the digital space but impacts real-life relationships. It is how their world works, and increasingly how the world works. For the most part, older generations do not know what this means for the next generation.

Mental health concerns. With the arrival of Gen Z came a wave of mental health issues and crises. Many studies show a rise in mental health issues that began in 2012, while the oldest members of Gen Z were young teenagers.[7] This rise follows the same trajectory as adolescent access to smartphones and social media. Often in conversations I am met with surprise and shock when I mention Gen Z's mental health issues began before the Covid-19 pandemic. The pandemic highlighted and exacerbated what was already happening. During the Covid-19 pandemic, anxiety tripled and depression quadrupled in adults, but disproportionately affected young adults.[8] It brought visibility, and I think some understanding, among older generations as we all experienced life on screens for a while.

The following are just a few stats around mental health and Gen Z. Most of these studies were done when Gen Z was in middle school or high school, and they are impacted by those experiences into adulthood. It is the context in which they have grown up and helps us understand where they are coming from. Their generational context is a constant conversation around mental health, and for good reason:

- Suicide rates for those aged 15–19 doubled from 2010 to 2020, but suicide rates for those aged 10–14 tripled from 2007 to 2018.[9]

- 20 percent of adolescents ages 12–17 had a major depressive episode in 2022, and 1 in 15 made suicide plans.[10]
- 47 percent of young people say they are moderately or extremely depressed, 55 percent say they are moderately or extremely anxious, and 45 percent say they are moderately or extremely lonely.[11]
- Gen Z is the loneliest generation in the United States,[12] and adolescent loneliness has risen globally in thirty-six countries since 2012.[13]
- Declines in adolescent happiness, life satisfaction, and flourishing, as well as increases in loneliness, anxiety, and depressive symptoms since 2010 have been linked to the increasing popularity of smartphones and social media around this same time.[14]

Can we agree that something is wrong? This isn't kids being kids or a generation being over-dramatic. They are suffering, and we must pay attention. This isn't limited to the United States or Western, English-speaking countries. Mental health struggles are popping up globally for the same age group, Gen Z. The reasonable next question to ask is: *What do they have in common?* Experts like Dr. Jean Twenge have answered with *technology*.[15] Many are surprised to find the presence and ubiquitousness of technology in so many corners of the world, connecting Gen Z through digital and social media. Bobby Gruenewald, in a conversation for the YouVersion Bible app, shared that it is actually easier to get digital Bibles through smartphone apps to remote parts of the world than paper ones. The international news outlet France 24 reported millions of Filipinos are playing online games to earn income through cryptocurrency.

Whether or not a particular member of Gen Z has struggled with mental health, they certainly know someone who does. They are not untouched by the mental health statistics even if they are not a statistic themselves, and this impacts their values, experience, and worldview. As they have grown up, they have navigated social media, active shooter drills and school shootings, and a global pandemic. All of these are unique to Gen Z's specific time of adolescence. They bring a new and different perspective to life and faith that, if we let it, adds value to the life and faith of all generations. It is our task today to understand how, so that by drawing these things out, Gen Z can reflect the kingdom of heaven the way they are designed to.

PURSUING GEN Z, NOT FIXING GEN Z

Each chapter will include four parts. First, it will present a question Gen Z is asking about life and faith. As mentioned earlier, these questions are based on the values, experiences, and worldview of Gen Z. Then, the chapter will discuss the generational context surrounding the question. This can include why it is being asked, how it is being asked, and why older generations may be misunderstanding the question or not even recognize it being asked. Third, each chapter will refer to a feature of a disciple, connecting the question with discipleship. Finally, each chapter will look at the life and ministry of Jesus Christ in conjunction with the feature of a disciple and question presented.

Through this process, we will explore a response to each Gen Z question that we can share through the gospel and discipleship. Of course, there is overlap between chapters. Ideas and conversation are not isolated to one question or feature of a disciple. The questions presented here are not clearly compartmentalized from each other, and the ideas in each chapter reach into other ones. Make those connections, flip between chapters, and draw out the integrated nature of the evangelism and discipleship of this generation.

There are no quick fixes to the deep and complex Gen Z experience. It would be a mistake to look for one. The purpose of our discussion is not to find an antidote to "fix" a generation or the issues they face. It is a pursuit to understand and enter the context of a generation, respectfully and compassionately, with the gospel of Jesus Christ.

My hope is that this is not simply an instruction manual, but a guidebook on the process to answer any of the questions our next generation brings to us. I hope that this process can be applied to different scenarios as we figure out how to introduce the next generation to Jesus Christ and help them grow in their faith.

The seven questions. What is Gen Z asking about life and faith? We are going to examine seven questions Gen Z is asking based on their generational values and worldview. These questions may not be easily verbalized by Gen Z, or even be on top of mind for them. Sometimes the deepest questions aren't, but are lying under the surface, shaping so much of who we are and what we believe. Of course, a generation is not limited to seven questions; there are always more questions.

These seven questions come out of a deep dive into understanding Generation Z. By identifying what is important to Gen Z, what they are facing, what they experience, the culture that surrounds them, and what they value, celebrate, or mourn, we can begin to understand how Gen Z navigates life.

Part of that navigation is asking questions related to their values and experiences.

The questions discussed here are a reflection of Gen Z's generational culture. They may not be new questions—some are timeless, and many of us have asked these questions in our lives. However, the context around these questions has changed, and that changes both how we understand the question and the response needed. These questions are not outside ideas applied onto Gen Z, but questions drawn out of how this generation is navigating, seeing, and experiencing the world. These questions are based on values, experience, and worldview.[16]

THE SEVEN QUESTIONS	
1. Is God good?	5. Can I trust you?
2. Am I enough?	6. What is true?
3. Will you accept me?	7. Am I safe?
4. Do all people matter to God?	

It is tempting to quickly read and interpret each question from our own generational lens, but this would be a critical mistake. Each question is influenced by specific generational experiences and context. In this book, we will delve into the generational environment that cultivated Gen Z's questions. If older generations do not understand the context and purpose of the question, or even the linguistic nuances and meaning of the question, we will not be able to answer them, which is what has been taking place in our churches and ministries, as well as in our homes. Without understanding the questions Gen Z is asking, older generations of Christians are providing irrelevant and flawed answers, perpetuating the disconnect between themselves and Gen Z.

This, right now, is an opportunity to slow down and listen to the experiences and ethics, hopes and hurts, and curiosities and convictions of the next generation. It is when Gen Z is heard and understood by older generations that older generations can have meaningful conversations with Gen Z relating to the gospel and faith.

The features of a disciple. Part of our job as pastors, ministers, parents, and mentors to Gen Z is to help them figure out what it means to be a disciple of Christ. We get to look at Gen Z and consider how they can live in the way God designed them to reflect his image here on earth. That's why each chapter will pair a feature of a disciple with the question presented. Seven features of a disciple (Follower, Prophet, Steward, Forgiver, Neighbor, Worshiper, and Witness) are drawn from Kathleen A. Cahalan's work in *Introducing the Practice of Ministry*.[17] I added an eighth feature of a disciple to this list: Intercessor. Each feature is connected intentionally with a specific question Gen Z is asking. In some cases, it is because the question and the feature of a disciple engage the same values. In others, it is because the feature of a disciple helps to provide the answer to the question, or a landing place in the complexity of the question. It offers a change in the worldview from secular and fragmented to one centered on Christ.

The goal is to connect the dots between the questions Gen Z is asking and the life of a disciple, revealing a faith that is relevant and meaningful to their generational experience as we share the good news in evangelism and discipleship. They are not connecting the dots on their own. We have to work at making those connections for Gen Z. Let's explore how Gen Z can engage their generational values and experiences in a way that reflects the kingdom of heaven.

The example of Jesus. No conversation around the gospel and discipleship is complete without looking at the life and ministry of Jesus Christ. It is God incarnate, in the person of Jesus Christ, who not only speaks the gospel and teaches about being a disciple, but also models it. We can take the questions Gen Z is asking and look at gospel encounters with Jesus through that Gen Z lens and see what comes to light! Each chapter invites us to answer Gen Z's questions with the life and ministry of Jesus and practical discipleship. This helps make connections between the Christian faith and everyday life in a meaningful way. By entering into this practice, we can demonstrate that God is not irrelevant and disconnected, but in fact very relevant to the values, questions, experiences, and needs of our Gen Z friends.

READY, SET, GO!

Get ready to be comfortable being uncomfortable. We are entering into a crosscultural practice of contextualization. It means putting down our lens and picking up another we are not familiar with. I can say from my experience, it has developed a deep compassion and appreciation in me for Gen Z and their courage, creativity, and much more. It has deepened my passion for Gen Z. I have gained a deeper love of the Bible and awe of the gospel as the good news for all people. I have gained a new appreciation and perspective on the kindness of God, who reaches people within their cultural contexts in their own moments of time, and it has drawn me to a deeper level of worship. I hope this journey is not only about loving and caring for Gen Z, but also about our own personal gospel and discipleship journeys.

KEY IDEAS

Ask Gen Z: What have you heard about your generation from older generations or the media?

> **Gen Z asks:** Is God good? Am I enough? Will you accept me? Do all people matter to God? Can I trust you? What is true? Am I safe?

Response: Take some time to understand the experiences, values, and worldview of Gen Z to better see their perspective on matters of life and faith.

> **Result:** Open communication between generations creates opportunities for gospel and discipleship conversations.

2

IS GOD GOOD?

I sent a text to a Gen Z young professional: "Do you think God is good?"

He works full time about a mile from my house and has battled cancer the last couple of years. We opted for a brief interview over text.[1] He responded, "I would say, as a blanket statement, yes. Because if he's not good, then what is he? Bad? He just is? Which I disagree with. Therefore, I'd say he's good." He continued, "BUT if the statement was, 'God is always good,' I would probably push back. That one is a little tougher for me." I leaned back to consider his words. They not only reflected the pain of his journey, but also Gen Z's wrestling with the goodness of God.

To simply respond by saying good Trinitarian theology dictates God the Father, God the Son, and God the Holy Spirit can never cease to be good would not be a posture of really listening to his experience or appreciating his process. I would be slapping a theology Band-Aid on real-life pain.

I leaned in and texted, "Can I ask one more question? How would you define what is 'good'?" About ten minutes later, he responded, and his text began, "That's a tough one because

I think 'good' is so subjective." The subjectivity of the term *good* is partially what makes this such a difficult question to respond to with our Gen Z friends.

Karma, Santa Claus, the Secret, and even the prosperity gospel share similarities. If you do the right things, good things are manifested. Put out good vibes, and good vibes will come to you. Be faithful, and you will be rewarded. These systems make sense. There is a flavor of justice behind them. It is no wonder, though, when Gen Z faces suffering, hardship, obstacles, loss, or injustice, it is difficult to reconcile the idea of a good God with the reality that surrounds them. And it comes as no surprise when I sit across Gen Zers who have shared statements like these:

- "I could never believe in a God who would let my mom die."
- "How could my miscarriage be 'part of God's plan'? What kind of God would make that happen?"
- "I don't think God is kind. He does things that are mean."

Wherever each person is, and whatever the experiences of suffering—death, injustice, loss, obstacles, and so on—they have faced, Gen Z is left asking this question: *Is God good?*

It's often the first question I come across with our next generation. (I'm not sure this is the most important question to Gen Zers, but it is top of mind when given the opportunity to ask questions about God.) The question *Is God good?* is not necessarily expressed in these exact words (more on that later), but it is commonly presented as a reason not to believe in God. It lives in the hearts of our next generation, and it is the hardest question for me to respond to. The goodness of God has been questioned for ages. The serpent in the Garden of Eden persuaded Eve to question God's goodness, convincing her God had not told her the whole truth (Genesis 3:4-5).

There are a few reasons it is difficult to answer the question *Is God good?* Okay, there are more than a few reasons, but here are some: First, a natural consequence of living in an individualized society is that it's full of people with individual ideas of what is good. With a myriad of definitions of what goodness is, it becomes difficult to have a single agreed-upon meaning for what *good* means, especially looking at the character and actions of God. Either we or our Gen Z audiences must make massive value, worldview, and logic shifts to have the same conversation. I'm asking Gen Z to change or let go of how they define goodness to have the conversation, and that is a big request.

Second, this question asks to see and understand the thoughts and reasons of God. We either want to be brought up to the level of divinity to understand his goodness, or we want God to shrink down to fit into our idea of goodness. These are impossible or unreasonable tasks. Honestly, I'm not sure any answer would satisfy.

That brings me to my third reason. There is no easy response to honor a question that represents the depths of our hearts. Easy answers and simple formulas are cheap and unsatisfying. To wave off our Gen Z friends by responding, "Yes, of course God is good," is to dismiss their experiences, questions, and context. Our Gen Z friends deserve more than that. It is time for us to lean in, ask more questions, and be *with* our Gen Z friends in their experience. In *The Spiritual Lives of Young African Americans*, Almeda Wright shared, "What they *believe* about God is not fully addressing the situations they find themselves in."[2] This is not isolated to young African Americans, but is true for most of Gen Z. This disconnect contributes to Gen Z not thinking belief in God is necessary to make sense of the world.[3]

I stepped on stage and faced a room of five-hundred Gen Zers after the unexpected death of a beloved college student and shared about Peter getting out of the boat and walking on water with Jesus (Matthew 14:22-31). I asked, "Why didn't God stop the storm? Why do bad things happen?" All eyes were locked on me, everyone holding their breath, waiting for an answer. To be honest, I was looking for an answer too. All I could say was, "I don't know," and continued, "All I know is that there was a storm, and Peter's options were to either grab onto Jesus, or fend for himself in the boat." Bad things happen, the storms don't stop, and we have the same options as Peter. I don't know the mind of God. I don't know why, and our Gen Z friends see us follow God in our lack of understanding.

We can be *with* them.

We can sit down next to them, feel with them, cry out with them, and be angry together with them, and in allowing the space for them to be honest, scared, sad, hurt, angry, and tired, we demonstrate what the goodness of God looks like. We can help them find the answer. We have to look at the context that surrounds the question of God's goodness.

A WALK WITH GEN Z

I like to ask Gen Zers this question: What are some questions your friends or other people your age are asking about God? I'd recommend anybody ask this question. We might be able to guess the questions that will come up, but that doesn't mean we don't ask the question. It is an invitation to be a part of the conversation, to bring doubts, struggles, and questions to the table.

I've asked young people what they are asking about God for a few years. I've asked individuals, small groups, and large ones, made up of both churched and unchurched Gen Zers. Two questions come up repeatedly.

The first is a request for evidence of the existence of God: *Can you prove God is real?* There are many volumes on this topic from thinkers like Lee Strobel and Sean McDowell, and sources like the Jude 3 Project. Though I will say when it comes to this question, Gen Z is looking for an experience with God to know he is real, not a logical apologetic or well-orated answer. In 2023, Springtide Research Institute published a report saying both religious and nonreligious young people valued the *experience* of the sacred as important.[4] Gen Z is about the experience of knowing God is real.

The second question is a summary of a lot of why questions. *Why didn't God stop this horrible thing? Why does God let bad things happen to good people?* These are summaries of the much more personal questions: *Why did my mom get cancer? Why did God let my friend die? Why did he make me go through so much suffering this year?* There is one underlying question behind all these questions: *Is God good?*

What Gen Z is really saying is, if God is good, then there must be some redemptive purpose to the pain and suffering we see and experience. If Gen Z believed God is bad, then this question would be irrelevant. Hardship and suffering from a bad source make sense. Gen Z would not need to ask why. (Recall my conversation with the young professional at the beginning of this chapter.) This is good news! On some level Gen Z understands God is good or is supposed to be good. If there is an understanding that on some level God is good, then there is a longing to see and understand what the good reason was for the hardship and suffering experienced and observed in the world around us.

I have wrestled with the goodness of God, especially in the death of a newlywed friend in a car accident with a faulty seatbelt, followed by the death of another dear friend at the hands of an aggressive cancer, leaving his wife and two small children behind. I cried out, "Why God? Why? I don't understand!" It is the question of why that asks, *Is God good?* After all, a good God would not have been so reckless, at least according to my understanding of what is good.

The why question often bubbles up from a place of pain. Each person has a unique story, with bumps and bruises that may be similar to someone else's, but never identical. Though two people can experience the same painful event, they do not experience pain the same way.[5] Be slow to judge the validity of the pain Gen Zers carry. We may not understand the source of their pain or how they carry it. We can make hurtful assumptions when we do.

Globally connected. We've likely heard the questioning of God's goodness before expressed in all the "why would God" questions listed here, as well as many more. We've likely asked these questions ourselves. They are timeless in nature. So what makes the context for Gen Z's question different from previous generations?

For Gen Z, this question is not just related to personal experiences, but to a global perspective. Their connection with technology through social media, streaming services, and other digital media has given them access to what is happening around the world at all times. Since a young age, they have been aware of suffering, injustice, war, and more on a global scale. They are not limited to what is shared on local news or in a printed newspaper the way I was. Gen Z is not only surrounded by technology in the present day but have also been connected to it throughout their childhood and adolescent years.

This created an environment in which young people have grown up exposed to too much globally: current events, conflicts, food insecurity, political strife, sex trafficking, violent injustice, and more, streaming into the devices in their hands. There is too much to keep up with. We are human after all, not designed to know everything, but Gen Z internalized a responsibility to know and be aware all the time.[6] According to Gen Z cultural values, to not be aware is to be irresponsible and part of the problem.

Mental health concerns. Gen Z's experience with mental health influences the question of God's goodness. While the Covid-19 global pandemic is often blamed for the rise in poor mental health, and did indeed exacerbate it, rising anxiety, depression, and loneliness were already well-documented before 2020. Yes, there has been a lot of discussion around Gen Z and mental health.[7] The goal here is to figure out how mental health either influences or is influenced by the question *Is God good?* After all, if God is not good, is there hope? If there is no hope, anxiety, depression, and loneliness are predictable outcomes. Let's consider how understanding the mental health context of Gen Z impacts how we can respond to the question *Is God good?*

I already know I'm anxious. I was meeting with a Gen Zer for coffee. I almost always bring a book with me to read in case the person I am meeting is running late or will miss our coffee date altogether. I was reading Jonathan Haidt's *The Anxious Generation* when she walked in. I asked her what she thought when she saw a title like this referring to her generation. She shrugged and said, "I already know I'm anxious." I am no longer surprised when I hear a Gen Zer say, "I have anxiety." After all, close to half of young people struggle with some level of anxiety.[8]

Lazy or depressed? Depression among adolescents has been on the rise since 2012, when the oldest members of Gen Z were teenagers. One way this is identified is by measuring responses to statements like "I can't do anything right," "I don't enjoy life," or "My life is not useful."[9] The National Survey on Drug Use and Health has shown a 72 percent increase in persons aged 12–17 with major depressive episodes from 2012 to 2019 (before Covid-19).[10] Those are our young professionals now. What if Gen Z isn't lazy, but depressed?

Lack of sleep and physical isolation (not spending face-to-face time with people) increase the chances of becoming depressed.[11] Smartphones and social media are linked to Gen Z getting less sleep and fewer in-person interactions. From a fatigued and lonely place, Gen Z is asking, *Is God good?*

All by myself. Depression and anxiety go hand-in-hand with loneliness. A high school senior I know struggles with both anxiety and depression. He knows that showing up to one of our gatherings is good for him. He knows coming to a place where peers are gathered and the gospel is shared contributes to his overall health, not just spiritual health. Still, anxiety and depression have also prevented him from walking out the door of his home, and it was pretty normal for a leader to get a text from him saying, "I'm too anxious and depressed to come" or "My mental health isn't good, so I'm staying at home." Have you received that text?

Then, loneliness creeps in. The more anxiety one has, the more lonely one becomes, and the more lonely one becomes, the more anxiety one has.[12] It takes a lot of energy to intentionally break that cycle, and depression depletes energy. If we don't understand that, we don't understand how to meet our Gen Z friends where they are.

Gen Z is the most digitally connected and the loneliest generation. In a 2018 study, Cigna Group identified Gen Z as the loneliest generation in the United States.[13] Cigna Group followed up with their findings, and in 2023 conducted a study on Gen Z vitality.[14] While there was some improvement, they found Gen Z adults still struggle with loneliness and feeling disconnected from others, more so than any other American generation. In 2023, the United States Surgeon General identified an "epidemic of loneliness and isolation," with physical consequences.[15]

Loneliness is not just an American problem. In a sample of one million adolescents in thirty-seven countries, thirty-six out of thirty-seven countries had a rise in adolescent loneliness, and nearly twice as many adolescents displayed loneliness in 2018 than in 2012.[16] Again, this is all before the isolation of the Covid-19 pandemic shutdowns. It is from a lonely place Gen Z is asking, *Is God good?*

Mental health and the goodness of God. A rise in anxiety, depression, and loneliness corresponds with a rise in hopelessness. In the fear behind anxiety, Gen Z is asking, *Is God good?* In the hopelessness and fatigue of depression, they are asking, *Is God good?* In the isolation and despair of loneliness, they are asking, *Is God good?* In the confusion and anger of suffering, they are asking, *Is God good?*

Understanding Gen Z's experience with mental health, and how it frames their understanding of life, faith, and God, helps me to understand when and how to share the gospel. It provides a lens for what is good news. We can enter the conversation with the hope that endures, a hope that is an anchor for the soul (Hebrews 6:19). Connection to a higher power helps mental health.[17] Wouldn't it be fun to share this with a Gen Zer we care about? The relationship between faith and mental health is linked! Follow up with this question: *What if God created us to flourish with him and not apart from him?*

Ask some Gen Zers if they think God is good. In light of our earlier conversation, some may take the opportunity to say they don't believe in God. Others may respond with a quick yes, but not know why. Still others might get stuck on this question, wrestling with their experiences and what they believe good is. In every case, we get to become learners and listeners. There may be a temptation to provide an apologetic or theology that we believe answers their questions, but tread lightly here and listen to the Holy Spirit. When we ask a question, our primary work becomes to listen and understand.

THE SHORT ANSWER: IS GOD GOOD?

Who makes a good burger? What makes a good movie? What makes a good leader? Each response will be based on the individual's personal lens of what "good" means. *Is God good?* It all depends on your definition of good. At least, that's where most of us start.

Like many of us, Gen Z has their own ideas of what is right, good, and fair. This creates a filter through which they evaluate God and decide if God is good. *Good* is often defined by Gen Z as what makes one happy, satisfied, secure, accepted and well-liked, has only good outcomes, and is safe. For Gen Z, *good* often means there is no pain, no disappointment, no difficulty, no disagreement, and no sacrifice. In our conversation with Gen Z regarding God's goodness, it is necessary to have a clear definition of good, verbalized in concrete terms. We must make sure we are all speaking the same language to provide a meaningful and relevant answer.

How do we decide how to define what is good? First, we do not take our personal, individualized, or even cultural definition of good, and apply that to God to assess his goodness. We are not running God through our lens, our filter, our set of standards to assess whether or not God is good. We partner with our Gen Zers to look to God to define what is good. God is the source of goodness, as well as justice, mercy, love, and so on. You see, God *is* good, so we take our understanding of what is good *from* God. This is a difficult place to start with Gen Z, or with anybody. This requires the most help from the Holy Spirit. It is letting go of our understanding of good in order to adopt God's. That is a significant and challenging practice.

As pointed out earlier, Gen Z may have an understanding that *good* means a lack of what is hard, painful, uncomfortable, or costly to one's happiness or comfort. It only takes a brief scan of the Bible to see it is full of hardship, pain, discomfort, and sacrifice. Still, we have friends in the Bible with whom

Gen Zers can find fellowship and camaraderie as we walk with them to uncover together what *good* means. Pay attention to where Jesus is in the following passages.

Jesus calms the storm (Mark 4:35-41). Maybe we think a good God would have prevented the disciples from entering a storm. In hardship and fear, the disciples ask, "Don't you care?" After all, if Jesus cared, wouldn't he have prevented this situation? Seeing their circumstances, wouldn't Jesus be helping bail water, or at least be awake? The goodness of Jesus is not the prevention of the storm, but that he is *with* the disciples in the middle of the storm. God's *with-ness* is his goodness.

The death of Lazarus (John 11:1-44). When Jesus arrives after the death of Lazarus, both Mary and Martha greet Jesus with: "Lord, if you had been here, my brother would not have died." If Jesus had shown up, this hard, painful, costly thing would not have taken place, as if that event were absent of God. Maybe God didn't understand the assignment. How many times have any of us shared this sentiment? If God were here, this wouldn't have happened. The goodness of Jesus is not in preventing Lazarus's death, but in sharing in the grieving and weeping alongside others. Even though Jesus already had a plan to bring Lazarus back to life, he did not move past the reality of grief, but entered into it *with* Mary and Martha. Jesus wept. God's with-ness, even in mourning, is his goodness.

The criminals on the cross (Luke 23:29-46). One of the criminals crucified next to Jesus said, "Aren't you the Messiah? Save yourself and us!" He assumes a good God would prevent pain and suffering. When God does not, he yells insults in his anger. This is so relatable. It would be easy to think a good God would stop the pain, and then when he doesn't, we hurl our anger at God and conclude that God must be bad, powerless, or nonexistent, because a good, powerful, present God would stop pain. The criminal crucified on the other side of Jesus says, "Don't you fear God? . . . We are punished justly, for we are getting what our deeds deserve. But this man has done nothing wrong. Jesus, remember me when you come into your kingdom." This criminal recognizes that goodness exists outside of his personal knowledge and experience. His fear doesn't look like being scared of God, but respecting God as the source of justice, goodness, and even mercy as he requests for Jesus to remember him. The goodness of God was not to climb off the cross. Jesus is *with* those dying next to him, and in his experience, he is *with* all of us. His with-ness with us (and our with-ness with him) in Jesus' death was the good way, the only way we would be with him forever in paradise.

God's with-ness is his goodness. When we share the gospel with Gen Z, God's with-ness is what we draw out of these passages, explaining why it is good, how it reflects his acceptance of us (*Will you accept me?*) or why we can trust him (*Can I trust you?*). God did not prevent hard, painful, or even unjust things from taking place, but is with us in the midst of it. Jesus is Immanuel, God with us, and that is good. He invites us, saying, "Come, follow me" (Matthew 4:19).

To follow someone, we have to be with that someone. In God's with-ness with us, we witness what is good. In our with-ness with God, we can become a disciple who follows God. Yes, God is good, but we get our best understanding of what is good as we follow Jesus.

FOLLOWING THE LEADER

A disciple of Jesus Christ is a Follower of God. Part of being a disciple who follows God means seeing the triune God as the origin, definer, and teacher of all that is good, true, and fair. The Follower recognizes that goodness is not defined by ourselves, but by God. This is a new perspective and paradigm shift for Gen Z (okay, it is a shift for all of us!). As a disciple, we learn to follow God, and we embrace God as the ultimate source of all that is good.

Living as a Follower of God does not mean I will understand the ways of God, but it does mean I will trust God in my lack of understanding. In Phoenix, Arizona, lies the Canaan in the Desert prayer garden. It includes a desert pathway with stations of the cross portrayed in artful carvings out of stone. I have spent many hours there in prayer and solitude with the Lord, and most of that time is at the first station. I rarely make it past that spot. This station is Jesus agonizing in prayer in the Garden of Gethsemane. Next to the carving are the words "My father, I don't understand you, but I trust you." What an honest and surrendered place! Surrender is part of learning to be a Follower of Christ, to let go of needing to be in the mind of God, to have all the answers, and to know all the outcomes. It is putting my trust in the one who is leading me and learning to follow when I don't understand (*Can I trust you?*).

At the death of Lazarus, while Mary and Martha both greeted Jesus saying, "Lord if you had been here, my brother would not have died," Martha had a fuller conversation that reflected that she is a Follower of Christ. She makes three statements of faith:

1. "But I know that even now God will give you whatever you ask" (John 11:22).
2. "I know he will rise again in the resurrection at the last day" (John 11:24).
3. "I believe that you are the Messiah, the Son of God, who is to come into the world" (John 11:27).

Martha hopes God will raise her brother today, and she also knows her brother may not be raised until the last day. Her faith is in Jesus, the one she follows. She believes in God's goodness as a promise keeper and truth teller. She shows what it means to be a Follower of God: she has an idea of what she thinks is good, but puts that aside to follow the goodness of Jesus. Consider walking through this passage with some Gen Zers, asking them about Martha's process. Ask where they see themselves in her journey, and where they want to be. Ask them, "What do you think it was like for Martha to go through that process?"

Growing as a Follower of God is learning to understand that God defines goodness. It means denying the reflex to judge God, and learning how to judge what is good through God. This takes practice. At least in my own life, I have to practice how to take my own ideas of what I think is good or best and repeatedly surrender those to God's will. Sometimes I have to say it out loud or write it down. It is a dying of ourselves and our own ideas of what is good, or even best. We can look at Jesus for how he demonstrates what it means to be a Follower of God.

JESUS AS FOLLOWER

I mentioned before that it is not easy to become a Follower of God. There are times the Bible likens this process to death (but resurrection comes)! We can look at Jesus to see what it looks like to grapple with our own ideas of what we want and what we think is good while also being a Follower of God.

When Jesus takes his disciples to Gethsemane to pray (Mark 14:32-34), he describes how he is feeling to Peter, James, and John, saying "My soul is overwhelmed with sorrow to the point of death." Jesus is distressed, troubled, and overwhelmed to the point of death. From what I gather, many Gen Zers can relate with Jesus in this moment: distressed, troubled, and overwhelmed. They have a Savior who relates with them.

If we jump ahead, we also see Jesus was left alone in his distress. After telling his closest friends how he felt, they fell asleep while Jesus prayed (Mark 14:35-41). They could not be there for Jesus the way I think most of us would want our friends to be there for us. Again, I think so many in Gen Z resonate with Jesus walking through the relational isolation and loneliness they feel. It is from this distressed, troubled, overwhelmed, and lonely place a generation is asking, *Is God good?*

Jesus asks God for something different than he is about to face: "*Abba*, Father, . . . everything is possible for you. Take this cup from me" (Mark 14:36). I am all too familiar with praying that prayer: "God, please, take this circumstance, this pain, this hardship away." In the next moment, Jesus demonstrates what it means to be a Follower of God, taking it one step further. He follows his request with, "Yet not what I will, but what you will" (Mark 14:36).

Jesus laid down what he wanted and replaced it with God's will. Jesus recognized God's will is good, better than the human will. This is what a Follower of God learns to do. Jesus prayed this more than once (Mark 14:39). We might go to God more than a few times to wrestle with what we want and what we think is good, in order to fully surrender our request to God's will. It takes practice.

The crucifixion provides a framework for understanding the goodness of God as compared to what seems good from a human perspective. I can only imagine what Jesus' followers experienced between Jesus' death and resurrection and all the why questions that would have been asked to and about God. After Jesus' death, the disciples hid. Fear, fatigue, worry, grief, anger . . . all these could contribute to hiding.

On this side of the resurrection, I see the cross was necessary for the saving of myself and all who believe. It was the way God decided to accomplish victory over death and sin, so we can be with him. This was not a bad dad who sent his son to go on an errand of death for him. The triune God made this plan: God the Father, God the Son, and God the Holy Spirit made a way when there was no way. But in those moments of the suffering and death of Jesus, his disciples and friends must have felt like God the Father was disinterested, powerless, or absent, and certainly did not fit the human lens of what is good. Can our Gen Z friends relate? I can imagine how difficult it would be to pray, "My God, I do not understand you, but I trust you."

Many ask, *Is God good?* in the middle of the story, in the midst of Holy Saturday, knowing only that the one they put their hope in died, and they are unaware or unsure that resurrection is coming. It is difficult to see the coming redemption amid suffering, but Jesus' death and resurrection demonstrate God's goodness in that it is coming.

A TALK WITH GEN Z

There is a reason this is a difficult question to answer, and it's a complicated conversation with our Gen Z friends. It asks for a completely counter-generational-culture response. It asks for a worldview shift. It asks them to release their own ideas of what is good. Becoming a Follower of God is dying to self. In conversations with Gen Z, be patient and recognize this is not a small, quick, or easy task. From my experience, it can be a lifelong process to learn.

It is denying ourselves to take up the cross and follow Jesus, losing our lives to be saved (Mark 8:34-35). There is a reason there is such painful imagery here. There is loss, and loss means pain. We should not hide this from our Gen Z audience. We shouldn't sugar-coat the decision to follow Jesus Christ. If we are not honest about this, we prove ourselves not to be trustworthy. Following God costs everything. Let's face it, though, and help our Gen Zers face it: we are dying already. Under the weight of all we see, experience, and carry, many are dying, whether they are being crushed by mental health or the unjust systems in this world.

According to their own generational values, Gen Z is supposed to fight for justice, but not say any person or viewpoint is wrong. Gen Z is supposed to reject anyone who does harm, but accept everyone's values. They are supposed to stand against evil and wrongdoing without calling anything or anyone wrong. The task to make sense of what is good without a compass to do so must be incredibly stressful, confusing, and burdensome. Let's acknowledge this out loud to our Gen Z friends. We can show them that we see them in this confusion, and ask them if they want to hear about another option. I am not the ultimate authority on what is good; none of us are. Defining good is a God-sized burden we weren't supposed to carry.

On the other side of becoming a Follower of God, there is peace. It is peace that comes from hope in Christ that the kingdom of heaven is both here and coming, that death will not have the final word, and that God is not reckless with our lives. We do not have a reckless God, but an intentional and providential, loving and intentional, wise and merciful God, who has purposes beyond my understanding.

We can remind our Gen Z friends that this doesn't mean we can't ask God questions, or even wrestle with him. They can approach the throne of grace with all of their questions, protests, sadness, suffering, and anger. Following God is not letting those things come between them and God. It might even be turning to God and saying, "I do believe; help overcome my unbelief!" (Mark 9:24). We don't follow God because we have all the answers. Gen Z needs to know we don't have all the answers. They need to hear us say, "I don't know," and then watch us follow God.

While this question is a difficult one to wrestle with, it is an important journey to be on with Gen Z. Becoming a Follower of God is where we take our first step.

KEY IDEAS

Ask Gen Z: What are some questions your friends or people your age are asking about God? Do you think God is good? How do you define what is good?

Gen Z Asks: Is God good?

Response: Our definition of what is "good" is to be defined by God, who is the source of all that is good. The goodness of God is in his with-ness.

Result: We become a Follower of God through Christ. Our understanding of what is good comes from God. As a disciple, we learn how to engage with the suffering, hardship, and injustice through God.

3

AM I ENOUGH?

"What if I'm not enough?"

I was standing in a room with over three hundred young adults at Young Life's new-staff training. These young men and women had collected to prepare for vocational ministry. There was palpable excitement, passion, and energy in the air, as one would expect in a room full of Gen Z twentysomethings. I was leading a conversation around gospel proclamation to adolescents, and as we talked about the cross and atonement, I asked the room about different responses teenagers today could have. A hand raised, and the words came out, "What if I'm not enough?" At that moment, I realized he wasn't just asking a question on behalf of teenagers, but for himself. I felt the question hang in the air and the resonance of those words spread throughout the room as I looked into the eyes of these young adults, full of fear and hope.

These were young adults who had chosen ministry. In many ways, we look at them as success stories. They made it through adolescence! They are adults who believe in and follow Jesus! They are active disciples of Christ! And I can (and have) quickly shoved them into the category of "I don't have to worry about them anymore," and turned my attention to those I think are more visibly in need of the good news. But here they were, asking the question *Am I enough?* Enough of what? Enough for what? Enough for who? What is really being asked? How was I going to answer this question?

Gen Z's question of being "enough" is often misunderstood by older generations, especially older generations of Christians, who often associate the idea of being "enough" with the question of being righteous enough or holy enough in the presence of a righteous and holy God. For previous generations of Christians, enoughness was discussed and measured in conjunction with sin. Of course, we are not righteous enough to earn our love or value, as we are depraved in the face of righteousness: "For all have sinned and fall short of the glory of God" (Romans 3:23). That is only one lens through which to see the question *Am I enough?*

If we are quick to answer our Gen Z friends with such a response, we ignore the generational context of their question. We give them an answer that doesn't match what they are *really* asking: *Am I enough to be loved or valued? What do I need to do for God to love me?*

Allow me to present this question in a different way, a contextualized way. Picture a young child standing in front of a parent. The child, nervous, vulnerable, and sincere, looks up at the parent and timidly asks, "What do I need to do to earn your love? Who do I need to be for you to love me?" It would seem unkind, even preposterous, to qualify that answer with, "I'm sorry, you will never be worthy of my love, but I love you anyway." Such an answer could crush a child. Instead, we would expect a parent to answer with, "Nothing, because I already love you completely! You never need to do anything or become someone different to earn it!"

Yet, when Gen Z asks if they are enough for God to love and value them, many older generations of Christians provide a response, almost like a theological reflex: *No, you are not, but God loves you anyway.* The theological sentiment behind the words may be true in part; God loves us despite our sin and a parent loves a child regardless of their deeds. This response does not take into account how or why the question is being asked. It is a standardized answer that misses the mark of responding to the heart of the question our Gen Z audience is asking. The heart of the question is, *Does God love me?*

According to a global survey conducted by Young Life, 41 percent of Gen Z globally (46 percent of Gen Z in the United States) is not confident they are worthy of being loved.[1] Let me say this one more time because it is just too critical to the conversation to ignore. On average, four out of ten Gen Zers globally are not confident they are worthy of being loved, and they are bringing that into adulthood. Not only are they questioning whether they have value or are lovable, many have decided they are not. With that in mind, do we see how important our response is to the question *Am I enough?*

Many of us from older generations will need to learn to step away from our own lens and experience to prevent providing a biased, irrelevant, or even wrong response to this question. We can start by asking a Gen Z friend: How do you define what being "enough" means?

A WALK WITH GEN Z

Digital culture, namely social media, provides a framework for Gen Z's worldview around the question *Am I enough?* The current culture of social media, as well as other digital media, emphasizes status, success, and competition, all measured by metrics like reposts, likes, comments, and shares. Social media offers an addictive reward system, causing the brain to respond the same way to receiving "likes" as it would to winning money or eating chocolate.[2] No wonder Gen Zers can fall into the trap of chasing and collecting "likes" as a way to measure, validate, or create self-worth. Who doesn't like affirmation or encouragement? Who doesn't like to be liked? Without a system for measuring likeability and success, how do I know if I am likable and successful?

Social and digital media offer variable reinforcement schedules. No one knows when the reward will come, which post will be liked, or which story will be shared. This lack of fixed pattern and predictability often keeps Gen Z (and let's face it, other generations) tied to social and digital media anticipating the next reward. That is only part of the picture. The impact of this trickles down to a deeper level.

In the CBS report, "Are the Kids Alright? The Internet," nineteen-year-old Emma said, "The most harmful possible thing you can give to a child, in my opinion, is a device that can quantify their worth through likes and comments."[3] She goes on to explain that young people exhaust themselves trying to obtain or accomplish something that is unattainable, unrealistic, and ultimately doesn't exist. This reveals an intriguing aspect of Gen Z: they are aware of the false reality, but still are drawn to chase it.

Consider how this can play out. A young man posts a photo at the gym, flexing larger-than-life biceps and sculpted abs with the caption "no days off." The posted photo garners numerous likes and positive comments of praise, including admiration from girls. Other young men viewing the post, and responses to the post, come to this conclusion: *In order for me to be valued and loved, I have to look like that.* This solicits extra workouts at the gym or a change in diet. Conversely, it could also create a sense of defeat as a disheartened young person thinks, *I'll never look like that, so I won't even try, and I'll never be loved or valued.* Meanwhile, the photo was likely altered, edited, and photoshopped to create an image that was not real to begin with. What was the impact of this false reality on a generation as they grew up?

The never-ending chase for self-worth. The social and digital media cultural system offers both public affirmation and punishment. It has created a quantifiable method of measuring one's own worthiness or worthlessness to be loved or valued. Social media feeds are flooded with high-performing, elite individuals, even peers, perpetuating the need to always have another achievement or accomplishment to keep up with others and prove self-worth.

In high school, I competed in the 800-meter run. I was a decent athlete, performing well amongst my peers in my school and region. Those were the only runners to compare myself to—the ones I saw in-person. Today, a high school track athlete is not limited to comparing themselves with those in their geography, but around the world. Being a decent athlete at one's school is trampled by better, even exceptional, peer performances from around the world. Because social media normalizes elite performances, it skews self-perception, redefining what was once a decent performance to one of absolute mediocrity, communicating, *You are not enough.* Suddenly, the race time that once elicited excitement now fosters disappointment.

Let's go back to my high school running career. Every race was an opportunity to set a personal record, to run faster than I had ever run before. Over the years in high school, I shaved off seconds and then tenths of seconds, improving my race. It fueled my competitive nature. I was always chasing a faster time, an appropriate mindset for an athlete. As I've aged, I've lost the physical ability to set a new personal record for the 800-meter run. That is reasonable, expected, and, dare I say, normal. I had to learn to gain satisfaction and meaning outside of a competitive time. I had to learn I had value as a runner outside a particular pace. Otherwise, I could lose myself in a never-ending chase for an unrealistic, false reality.

This is the place we find Gen Z. Without a sense of identity and value, they find themselves in a race, where no matter how long or fast they run, the finish line keeps moving farther away, or even changes in direction. In their exhaustion, the question of enoughness presents itself: *When will I be enough?*

Social and digital media have impacted Gen Z regarding identity formation, mental health, and relationships, culminating in the question, *Am I enough to be loved or valued?* Social and digital media are far too quick to repeatedly communicate this message to Gen Z: *You are not enough.* This is the context that has surrounded Gen Z. Three-fourths of high school students interviewed for *Three Big Questions That Change Every Teenager* mentioned being "not enough" in their interviews.[4]

This is not just a teenage problem, as many Gen Zers are adults and have made the move from comparing prom dresses to comparing careers. This is how Gen Z learned to navigate the world and figure out who they are: by looking for an answer to their question *Am I enough?* It informs how they navigate adulthood.

Failure and identity formation. Identity formation does
not happen in a vacuum, but in relationship to others. For
Gen Z, accomplishments and successes are important to
personal identity. This also means failures and mistakes are
guiding forces for defining personal identity. Whether the
discussion is around success or failure, both are done in relationship to others: competition, comparison, and community.
A young woman is called kind in comparison to others' apathy
or lack of kindness. A young man is called smart in comparison
with others' test scores. Personal characteristics are often identified by judging others. The digital space offers "a wide range
of choices" for Gen Z by presenting many different identities
on curated social media feeds.[5]

For Gen Z, each accomplishment or lack thereof becomes
a mile marker on the journey of identity formation. This puts
a tremendous amount of stress and weight on each moment,
step, and decision of their journey. For Gen Z, failure is not
a part of the journey or a natural learning process; it is an
identity marker. Failure is not an obstacle to learn from or
move through; it is a signpost of a fixed characteristic. Failure
is not given room as an opportunity for growth and development; it closes doors to hopes and dreams. For Gen Z, failure
tells them who they are not.

With such high stakes, it is no wonder failure or the risk
of failure would be avoided at all costs. Any measurable successes and accomplishments would be welcomed to replace the
lingering despair from personal shortcomings or anticipated
failures. Why risk failing and finding out I'm not enough? Can
we see why our Gen Z friends are stressed out? With so much
at risk with every step or misstep, I would be afraid to take any

steps! Gen Z has much more courage and strength than they are given credit for!

She unfollowed me. Relationships are intertwined with Gen Z's experience in the digital world. Gen Z generally expects some level of digital engagement and sharing; it is their cultural norm. Social and digital media spaces are public forums made up of people (and bots impersonating people). Gen Zers are aware that every word, picture, action, or inaction incites response. Every single one. Nothing goes unnoticed or unpunished. When a Gen Zer presents an aspect of his or her personality through a sentence, caption, picture, or video, it is offered to the community for its consideration.

The response, or lack thereof, informs the Gen Zer if he or she is valued or loved in that moment. They see what was shared or rejected, corrected, or even not worthy of any attention. The more aspects of one's personality, accomplishments, appearance, or ideas are liked, re-shared, and affirmed through comments, the more identity can be formed around those things. These are the characteristics that have been identified as lovable and valuable in relationship with others.

The inverse is true also. The more aspects of one's personality, accomplishments, or ideas are mocked, called out, shut down, or ignored, the more identity can be formed without those things. Through a system of retweets, likes, shares, stitches, and comments provided by social and digital media, Gen Z has been able to form their identities in a public and global forum of comparison. All of this contributes to the context of the question *Am I enough?* Am I enough for you to love me and think I have value? Am I enough for you to be my friend?

Gen Z has experienced the formation and destruction of relationships in the online community forum. It is easy to end relationships. Just "ghost" them (stop responding and ignore them).[6] Digital relationships are conditional and disposable, but this also extends to in-person relationships. With a click, one can be unfollowed, blocked, or deleted from a relationship without any conversation or face-to-face interaction.

In a conversation with a college student, I asked about a friend of hers, to which she responded, "We aren't friends anymore. She unfollowed me." Confused and not understanding the social structures of her generation, I asked follow-up questions about any conversations or in-person interactions they had. I was applying my generation's cultural context to this friendship. This time, she increased her volume, slowed down her speech, and over-enunciated her words: "SHE UN-FOL-LOW-ED ME!" Clearly, I had not understood the social, generational structure she lived in, but when she said those words to me, I realized that the simple click of the "unfollow" button communicated more than enough in their generational language. I had to step back and recognize there were different cultural rules for Gen Z, ones that contribute to the question of enoughness.

These kinds of terminations in relationships happen on a regular basis for Gen Z. Conditional friendship reinforces the need to be enough. Gen Z is sharing about who they are, offering it up to the digital community, and waiting to be either embraced or shut down. Behind each offering of themselves is a question of whether or not they will prove to be enough. More often than not, the digital community does not offer the desired encouragement or embrace, resulting in the message, *You are not enough to be loved or valued.*

This question of enoughness not only influences how Gen Z engages and views the world and others around them, but how they engage with or view God.

No room for error. I was meeting with my tutor to help me with my homework while in seminary, fumbling my way through ancient Greek. My tutor pointed out a mistake I had made in my grammar, and I began to erase furiously with vocal expressions of my frustration and embarrassment. He gently put his hand on my paper and kindly said, "That's okay. That's how we learn." He made room for mistakes. Mistakes didn't mean I was doomed to fail in ancient Greek (though that was my last Greek class). Mistakes are expected on the journey of learning and even in the mastery of a subject.

Gen Z did not and is not growing up in a time that allows this kind of philosophy around making mistakes. Their cultural context demands perfection. The social media community that makes up the public forum has been placed in a seat of judgment. Each user, screen in hand, has been given a platform to observe and listen to anything that is shared in the public digital forum and give unsolicited critique. Imagine navigating adolescence and identity formation in an environment that does not allow mistakes, or even forgiveness. Imagine how that would impact adulthood.

Gen Z has grown up watching ideas being shared, and, in real time, commended—retweeted and celebrated, or called out—rebuked and canceled. Gen Z has observed old photos or tweets from public figures unearthed from the past and used to destroy them in the present.

Gen Z knows this is not limited to having the wrong opinion, but extends to asking the wrong question, or even not knowing what to say or do, and making the wrong decision to be silent. This sociocultural pressure eventually becomes an obstacle to Gen Z asking questions or sharing any thoughts, fearing they could be met with hostility, outrage, and rejection. There is no hiding, unless they go into total isolation. It's no wonder anxiety and loneliness are prevalent, and why Gen Z keeps asking, *Am I enough?* With such unhealthy and destructive experiences with failure or rebuke, this also puts parents, supervisors, mentors, and pastors in a tough spot when correction is needed.

What if we put ourselves in the shoes of Gen Z? Imagine internalizing the idea that you are not loved, not lovable, and not worthy of being loved when the digital metrics don't meet your needs. Imagine hearing there is nothing about you that brings value to the world or those around you. In his book *Life of the Beloved,* Henri Nouwen wrote that it becomes easy to believe the voices in this world who are constantly shouting at us, "You are no good, you are ugly; you are worthless; you are despicable, you are nobody—unless you can demonstrate the opposite."[7] It would be reasonable to look inward and decide there must be something wrong with me. It is no wonder that a digitally native generation would struggle with mental health and feeling enough to have value or be loved.

THE SHORT ANSWER: AM I ENOUGH?

It is not what we do that makes us worthy of God's love; it is God's love that gives us value. In other words, we do not earn God's love by proving our value, but we are valuable because God loves us. By God identifying us as his beloved ones, he assigns value to us. By offering forgiveness, he assigns us an identity as his beloved ones. God the Father, God the Son, and God the Holy Spirit created a plan for redemption and restoration from the beginning. From the beginning, God decided: You are enough to be loved and valued. Henri Nouwen said the world will lie to us, "constantly trying to convince us that the burden is on us to prove that we are worthy of being loved."[8] Nouwen spends a whole book trying to convince the audience of the truth: we are beloved ones of God, and meant to live into knowing our identity as Beloved.

God's plan for atonement and redemption demonstrates his love for us. We need to tell our Gen Z friends they are valuable because God's love says so. Their identities are to be formed as ones forgiven and beloved. "God decided you are enough—you are his beloved one"—let's say this over and over to our Gen Z friends, and maybe to ourselves too. And when we think we have said it enough, we say it again. Write it on a piece of paper, send it in a text, create a calendar reminder, do anything to repeat this message multiple times in multiple formats. Be ready for rolled eyes, big sighs, and being brushed off accompanied by the "Yeah, you've said this already, and I already know." The contrary message has been too loud for too long, and it will take repetition to create a new habit for our Gen Zers to think, and then to believe this: *I am enough for God to love and value me. I am forgiven and beloved. I am enough because of Jesus.*[9]

Once that is decided, understood, and soaked in, the disciple can lean into the feature of Forgiver.

ENOUGH TO FORGIVE

The next challenge is to help our Gen Z friends have an outward expression of their enoughness in discipleship: become a Forgiver. At first glance, it may seem odd to pair the question of being enough with learning to forgive as one who is forgiven. It may make more sense to offer an identity as one who is redeemed, sanctified, or beloved. After all, these seem to answer the question *Am I enough?* While those traits reflect our vertical relationship with God, they stop short of our horizontal relationships with the world and others.

Being a Forgiver shows how a beloved and valued disciple can now minister to others. A disciple of Christ can recognize this: *I am loved and valued enough to offer forgiveness to others rather than look to others to fill a need for love and value!* When a disciple, secure in Christ, is no longer seeking love and value to fill an inner need, this filled-up disciple has something to give away.

To offer forgiveness, the Forgiver must be in a position of worth. A Forgiver is loved enough to offer love in the form of forgiveness. A Forgiver has value and can now offer value in the form of forgiveness. A Forgiver does not need anything from the one being forgiven. Being a Forgiver means knowing one is enough to forgive another. What a gift to offer Gen Z! Gen Z can develop an identity grounded in Christ and impact a deeply hurting world around them at the same time.

Recall the conversation about the role of successes and failures in identity formation for Gen Z. As we respond to Gen Z's question of enoughness in sharing the gospel, we invite them to learn to be a Forgiver, taking a different pathway to identify formation in discipleship. When they become Followers of God, Gen Z can take a deep breath and put down the burden of trying to figure out their identities through the noise of social and digital media.

Forgiveness does not use success and failure to decide one's own identity. Failure is not an identity marker! The existence of forgiveness not only makes room for failures and mistakes, but also expects them! When all is said and done, forgiveness only really exists in relation to failures and mistakes. If only success and accomplishment exist, and if only perfection exists, then there is no place for forgiveness. Being a Forgiver frees others from relying on a never-ending game of weights and balances to form personal identity or define self-worth. It says, *You are enough because God loves and values you.*

Learning to forgive equips Gen Z to bring good news to others. Forgiveness acknowledges the forgiven one is enough to be loved and valued by God. This is an important distinction from the Forgiver assigning love and value. The Forgiver submits to God in the act of forgiveness, acknowledging God is the one who assigns love and value. It is not the role of the Forgiver to assign such, nor to deny it. It is God's passionate and powerful love that provides redemption, restoration, and sanctification. By practicing forgiveness, the Forgiver actively steps out of the role of Judge. Rather than participating in critiquing or judging others, the Forgiver recognizes God as the Judge. Forgiveness affirms the belovedness of others. It is a horizontal expression of our vertically received love and value.

I'm still learning how to forgive. It can be overwhelming to think we are instructed to forgive one another as God has forgiven us (Ephesians 4:32). That challenge could frustrate our Gen Z friends as they see definite failure in meeting such a standard. Let's invite our Gen Z friends to learn alongside us, placing ourselves next to them as disciples who together learn what forgiveness means and how to engage with it. Let's invite our Gen Zers to join us in looking at Jesus. We can open up the passage discussed in the next section (John 8:1-11) together and draw out what it means to be a Forgiver, sitting side by side.

JESUS AS FORGIVER

While Jesus is teaching in the temple courts, a woman caught in the act of adultery is brought before Jesus and the assembly (John 8:1-11). Her sin is shared in a public forum, and the people quickly jump into seats of judgment. (Ask your Gen Z audience, "Doesn't that kind of sound like social media?") Here is a woman, whose failure is on public display, offered to a public forum all too eager to offer their flawed judgment. The teachers of the law and Pharisees take Scripture seriously, as should we. However, taking the Bible seriously should not equate to becoming judges of others in place of God. We can learn from observing Jesus as a Forgiver in contrast with the Pharisees and teachers of the law.

Only the woman is brought forth, and according to the Law, both parties, man and woman, are to be punished. With the absence of the man, the teachers of the law and Pharisees demonstrate their flawed place as judges. While they take Scripture seriously, they are neglectful in handling it. Let us be mindful that when we take on the feature of Judge (rather than Forgiver), our judgment will likely be erroneous, inaccurate, and distorted. Still, the Pharisees remind Jesus that the Law commands "to stone such women," and ask what Jesus has to say.

After writing on the ground with his finger twice, Jesus makes room for the prescribed penalty by setting a standard for the first person to throw a stone: perfect righteousness, to be without sin. This strips the position of Judge from anyone within the assembly except for Jesus; Jesus is the only one who has the right to throw the first stone. After everyone left, and only the woman and Jesus remained,

> Jesus straightened up and asked her, "Woman, where are they? Has no one condemned you?"
>
> "No one, sir," she said.
>
> "Then neither do I condemn you," Jesus declared. "Go now and leave your life of sin." (John 8:10-11)

Jesus does not ignore her sin, condone her sin, or say this woman did not sin. By saying he does not condemn her, Jesus forgives her sin. By telling her to leave her life of sin, Jesus acknowledges her sin, but her mistakes and failures do not define her identity. She is set free by forgiveness, loved and valued. There is no measurement of accomplishments and failures to decide if this woman was worthy enough to be forgiven. Jesus decided she is enough. Forgiveness was not offered because of who the woman was, but because of who Jesus is.

There is another layer of mercy that occurs in this passage. It's hard to see because it is so subtle. Rather than calling out the sin of the teachers of the law and Pharisees, Jesus also acknowledges their sin by saying anyone without sin can cast the first stone. He did not destroy them but let them walk away without certain and immediate punishment.

Jesus does not allow anyone to sit in his rightful seat as Judge, but as Judge he exemplifies how to be a Forgiver. While Jesus is indeed God and the source of all forgiveness, he also demonstrates what the life of a disciple looks like. He acknowledges sin and forgives it. It is not about how good or bad the receiver of forgiveness is. Forgiveness is offered by the ultimate Judge, who through the act of forgiveness assigns love and value to us.

As we look at this passage alongside our Gen Z friends, we explain how we all are reflected in the story:

- We are the Pharisees, too quick to jump into a seat of judgment, especially behind a screen, in a faceless crowd. What would it be like for our Gen Z friends to admit that their principles may be good, but their judgment may also be flawed? It may help for us to admit where we have been quick to offer distorted and mistaken judgment.

- We are the woman who was caught. Without Jesus, her mistakes would have led to death. If Gen Z lives in the judgment of the world, it leads to death: death of the soul, death of identity, death of mental health, and even physical death. She is set free by forgiveness and is not defined by her mistakes. She is enough to be accepted and forgiven by Jesus.

- We can be found in the actions of Jesus. As disciples, Gen Z can learn to forgive and show mercy like Jesus, in both obvious ways, like with the woman, and subtle ways, like with the Pharisees.

A TALK WITH GEN Z

For Gen Z, in growing up with constant judgment where failure is not an option, the process of forgiveness has rarely been observed. I asked some of my Gen Z friends to write step-by-step instructions on how to forgive someone, to create a concrete process for an abstract concept. Here are the steps they gave me:

1. Take a deep breath and calm down.

2. Pray—don't just go talk to someone who puts fuel on the fire.

3. Understand everyone is dealing with stuff we can't see. Give them grace.

4. Find a healthy way to deal with the hurt (ask a mentor for help with this).

5. If I start to get upset when I talk about it, start over again.

This is a good start! If I just took the first two steps, it would prevent a lot of stress and strife in my own life. Living as a disciple of Christ who is a Forgiver offers freedom. The idea that forgiveness is a pathway to freedom may be a totally foreign concept for Gen Z and must be explained from the perspective of their values, experience, and worldview.

First, practicing forgiveness removes the burden of sitting as a judge. Judgment does not place us *with* people but *against* people, deciding if each person is friend or foe, worthy of love and value, or worthy of punishment and rejection. Judging constantly observes endless incidents of failures and mistakes, and it attempts to weigh each one out to offer appropriate and necessary consequences for each incident and each person. It is a lonely place to live. This is how Gen Z is living right now. Freedom resides in recognizing God as Judge and trusting God's perfect judgment. We do not have the burden to judge.

Second, Forgivers acknowledge their identities as disciples of Christ, forgiven, beloved, and valued. No one can take that away. There is no need to chase the accumulation of successes and accomplishments to find personal identity; it is already decided. Failures and mistakes do not need to be given undue weight in identity formation. In Christ, sin has been conquered.

Being a forgiven Forgiver does not mean being perfect, but it allows Gen Z to face their own and others' imperfections with the tool of forgiveness in hand.

Third, forgiveness does not ignore the wrong, hurt, or violation, but acknowledges it. Forgiveness recognizes sin but removes the power of sin. Forgiveness gives Gen Z the freedom to see the image of God reflected by others (*Will you accept me? Do all people matter to God?*). Forgiveness gives freedom to the Forgiver to see God's love and righteousness in others.

Fourth, forgiveness does not deny justice. It is tempting to think forgiveness is the opposite of justice, and this can cause inner tension for Gen Z, who long for wrongs to be set right (*Is God good? Do all people matter to God?*). Forgiveness and justice are not opposing forces or mutually exclusive. As Forgivers, we can help Gen Z engage with both forgiveness and justice. In the cross, justice and forgiveness are present at the same time. The justice of God is fulfilled in the act of atonement, and forgiveness is offered to those who put their faith in him. The peace of forgiveness exists because God enacts justice. He sets things right, both condemning sin and offering freedom from condemnation.

While engaging in forgiveness is often an internal process that slowly takes place over days, weeks, months, and even years, it is important to share that process with Gen Z. Forgive out loud. Wrestle, grieve, process, go on walks, listen to loud music, ask questions, seek wisdom in Scripture, and pray in proximity to Gen Z friends. Let them see and experience what it means to be a Forgiver *with* us. This invites them to process forgiveness alongside us, and to see what freedom in forgiveness looks like.

KEY IDEAS

Ask Gen Z: How do you define what being "enough" means? What does it look like to forgive someone?

Gen Z Asks: Am I enough?

Response: God decided you were fully loved and valued from the very beginning, when he created a plan of atonement, redemption, and restoration for you. He loves you so deeply that he decided you were worthy of such a plan. You are valuable and loved because God said so.

Result: As one who is loved and valued by God, you extend love and value to others in the form of forgiveness.

4

WILL YOU ACCEPT ME?

I stumbled upon a welcome mat with the words, "All are welcome here." The notion behind these words is that *anyone standing at the threshold will find acceptance in this home.* I wondered why this statement needed to be on a welcome mat. Isn't the very essence of a welcome mat to welcome everyone into the place where it sits on the threshold?

This saying is an affirmation of a cultural value, one that has been instilled in Gen Z: acceptance. More specifically, it is acceptance of those who may have not been welcome in many places, who have been shut out or excluded. To say "all are welcome here" is a way to spit in the face of the patterns of societal and systemic rejection.

A WALK WITH GEN Z

Acceptance is a core generational value. Gen Z sees themselves as more open and accepting than previous generations. Pause and ask a Gen Zer what makes their generation different than previous ones. When I ask this question, the first response is often, "We are more open-minded and accepting." If it's not the first response, it's in the top three, revealing how important acceptance is to Gen Z.

In a study around stigma, Gen Z was more accepting than previous generations of people who identify as LGBTQ+, those living with a substance disorder, and those with nonnormative sexual histories.[1] Gen Z is more open and accepting of different people and different practices than previous generations. For example, Barna found Gen Z considers not recycling as morally worse than viewing pornography.[2]

Acceptance is a pathway to secure relationships. Maybe we all have asked the same question to others in our lives: *Will you accept me?* This could be personal or professional, in tryouts for a sport, applying for school or a job, or in moments where we have made a mistake and hurt someone else. In the throes of adolescence, while we are figuring out who we are and where we belong,[3] we have probably asked this question countless times. To feel accepted is a good thing. For others to feel accepted by us is a good thing. But what if acceptance looks different to different generations? What if our efforts to express acceptance only unknowingly perpetuate rejection?

I recently witnessed this dynamic between a Gen X supervisor and Gen Z employee. The supervisor thought acceptance was extended by listening to the ideas of the Gen Z employee. The Gen Z employee felt rejected because the Gen X supervisor did not communicate any intention to look into or execute any of the ideas, but simply told the Gen Zer to pick one and follow through with it. The Gen Zer felt punished for sharing ideas, and the Gen Xer thought encouragement through freedom had been extended. For the Gen Zer, acceptance meant the Gen Xer would like an idea so much, the supervisor would join in executing that idea. Weeks went by and frustration only built as the Gen Zer felt rejected and abandoned by the Gen X supervisor, and the Gen X supervisor felt the Gen Zer was not following through. Acceptance did not mean the same thing for both parties, and that miscommunication leaked into relational conflict.

Parlez-vous Gen Z? Do you ever feel like Gen Z is speaking a foreign language? Do you ever feel like you are talking with a Gen Zer, but the communication is jumbled, frustrating, or just plain confusing for both parties? Bruh, I hope you're vibing with the bars I'm spitting, no cap. Some think Gen Z is extra, full of sus randoms who need to touch grass, but they are fire. We are the ones who need a vibe check FR to get why the Christian faith gives Gen Z the ick.[4] This slang is probably already being replaced. But the barrier we may feel isn't really about slang, but about more complex and nuanced use of language.

Language gets us in trouble when we think we are saying one thing, but unknowingly saying something else. We may be using the same words as our audience, thinking we are speaking in the same terms, and we still aren't. Acceptance is one of those words that has different meanings to different cultures, generations, or even different individuals.

Gen Z and acceptance. From my experience, Gen Z values few things more than acceptance. Acceptance is tied to the other Gen Z questions discussed here around enoughness, safety, truth, trust, and the importance of valuing all people. Acceptance is a paramount value, core to human relationships, which means a misunderstanding of what it means to be accepted can unintentionally cause a rift.

This is where we begin to see the breakdown of communication when it comes to how we talk about God's acceptance of us. Gen Z understands acceptance through a specific cultural lens. However they experience the church discussing or displaying acceptance is not currently meeting Gen Z where they are. Gen Z concludes that the Christian faith is exclusive and full of rejection, and that either God is the source of this, and thus is a bad God, or that God is accepting, and thus the Christian faith is a bad faith.

We have to be careful in promising acceptance in the spaces we design and lead. If we say, "You will be accepted here," but we are not working within the definition of acceptance of our Gen Z audience, we can quickly and unknowingly break that promise. Then we will have proved ourselves to be hypocrites and untrustworthy. Can you see what is at stake here? If we do not lean in and understand the lens of our Gen Z audience, we can unintentionally fortify an obstacle between them and following Christ.

We are left wondering, *What does acceptance mean to Gen Z?* The value or idea of tolerance has become wrapped up into acceptance in recent history. While technically, acceptance and tolerance have different meanings, these terms are often used interchangeably. The Cambridge dictionary uses the word *accept* in its definition of tolerance: "willingness to accept behavior and beliefs that are different from your own, although you might not agree with or approve of them."[5] It is this last part of the definition that has been dropped in cultural use of the word tolerance. If forced to use the Cambridge definition, Gen Z will likely choose acceptance and reject tolerance.

Gen Z views themselves as more accepting of others than previous generations, especially of those who have been traditionally marginalized or rejected.[6] Gen Z's cultural context is full of opportunities to unknowingly or accidentally offend or reject others. They worry about unintentionally breaking their value of acceptance: *If I accidentally reject someone, I don't belong in the community of acceptance, and if I don't belong in the community, I'll be alone.*

Let's look at some ways acceptance is understood by Gen Z. They may not be totally foreign to our older generations, but let's pay attention to the subtle nuances of the meaning of acceptance from a Gen Z lens.

Acceptance is belonging. Acceptance is not merely being tolerated, but welcomed. It is finding a place where people are excited to see you, embrace you, and miss you when you are absent. It is feeling like you are a part of something bigger than yourself. Part of the adventure of adolescence is not only identity formation (who I am), but also figuring out friendships (where I belong).[7] This is the search for community. For many Gen Zers, belonging means feeling like they can relax and be their "authentic self." They do not need to change how they speak or interact, hide parts of their personalities, or be a different version of who they are. (This dynamic is often referred to as code-switching.) Acceptance means being fully seen and fully known, and then fully welcomed and embraced.

To be accepted is to be recognized, to have one's unique identity acknowledged in a positive way.[8] To be accepted is to belong, and to belong is to be accepted. I get to recognize and acknowledge what makes my Gen Z friends special. I'm smiling right now just thinking about it! I bet many of us recognize admirable, beautiful, incredible qualities unique to each of our Gen Z friends. Tell them right now—and make it specific to who they are! Recognition is seeing, and seeing is creating belonging, and belonging is acceptance.

It is painful for me to hear from a young person, "I don't belong here," especially if I contributed to the negative experience of disconnection or rejection. They do not see themselves as a part of the community. This contributes to loneliness as Gen Z processes: *If I am not accepted, I do not belong. If I do not belong, I do not have community. If I do not have community, I am alone.*

Belonging and acceptance are intertwined with each other but are interpreted by the individual. I can do my best to extend acceptance and belonging, but ultimately the accomplishment of that goal is in the eye of the beholder.

Acceptance is agreement. In Gen Z's lifetime, acceptance has been wrapped up with having the same opinions, beliefs, viewpoints, and principles. Disagreement can lead to feelings of not feeling seen or not being heard as expressions of not feeling accepted. Gen Z's cultural context dictates that if you do not agree with what I am saying or doing, then you do not accept me. This makes disagreement risky. It places landmines throughout both casual and close relationships. What if I say something my friend disagrees with? What if I say something my classmates disagree with? What if I don't agree with my friend? If acceptance is a core generational value, and acceptance is being in agreement with those around us, it makes Gen Z relationships vulnerable in conflict. It also limits social circles to either those who agree with each other or those who hide what they really think or feel, for risk of losing friendships.

I feel the risk of disagreeing with my Gen Z friends because of the convictions of my faith. I risk them rejecting me or feeling like I am rejecting them, all without a follow-up conversation or a relationship. They may feel rejected because they disagree with me. What if I instruct a Gen Zer not to cuss at a gathering? Will they feel rejected and never come back? The statement of compromise, "Let's agree to disagree," may still be used, but the underlying weight of it now says, "Clearly you don't understand or accept me, and I reject your ideas, so let's stop talking." It is the end of a relationship, not a truce to an impassable clash of ideas.

If we pause and take a step back, we notice Gen Z has come of age during a time when we haven't done disagreement paired with acceptance very well, especially in the public realm. We are being pushed to take sides, form tribes, and create an "us versus them" dynamic in political, theological, and social realms. In the media, we generally do not see examples of opposing views together in friendship. We don't see a heated debate followed by a meal shared together. We don't see arguments followed by expressions of mutual respect. How can we fault Gen Z for not understanding something that they have not seen modeled for them?

Acceptance means not asking you to change. Sometimes we can extend the question of acceptance by adding four words at the end: Will you accept me *for who I am*? This is a loaded and heavy question, and it races around all the time. In some cases, it is a statement more than a question: You *will* accept me for who I am.

It is the last part that is the kicker: for who I am. Why do the last four words add weight to the question? They can imply that my personality, my character, my appearance, my ethics, or anything about me is fixed, unmovable, and unchangeable.

This is who I am, rather than, *This is who I am in this part of my journey of growth.*

Discussions around sexuality generally include an expectation of not being asked to change. The term *sexual identity* binds sexuality to core identity: "This is who I am." According to Dr. Carl Trueman, inner spaces define identity, and if the inner space is primarily sexual, then limits on sex are viewed as limits on who we are.[9] Denying that core identity or asking for it to change (or be hidden as a form of change) breaks with Gen Z's value of acceptance. It is understood as a violation of identity, and that is unacceptable to Gen Z. Accepting the gender fluidity and sexual identity landscape was not a shift Gen Z had to make; it always was.[10]

Gen Z has internalized they are "never to be affected by any outside force that tries to shift my identity,"[11] especially if it doesn't *feel* like who I am. "I'm just a sarcastic person. This is how I am. It's how I show love, so you just have to deal with it." These words, stated in a matter-of-fact tone, were shared by an upperclassman as she faced our small-group Bible study. This young woman's statement did not create a place of acceptance but demanded permission to be mean without apology. Acceptance "for who I am" has created a system where I should never be asked to change, adjust, or be different. Acceptance means you have to deal with me the way I am. As you can imagine, this also becomes a barrier to deep friendships and relationships.

Somehow asking anyone to adjust, grow, change, or develop became an opposing force to acceptance. Now a generation has grown up seeing any request to adjust, grow, change, or develop as a point of rejection. It is as if they are saying, "You want me to be different than who I am, so you don't accept me for who I am." The words make sense, kind of, but it is incomplete logic. I accept you for who you are, *and* I support you in your journey to become who you are meant to be. That means growth and change. It does not mean I reject you; it does not mean I don't accept you. We are all on a lifelong journey of growth and change. To remain exactly the same our whole lives, even Gen Z would argue, is a problem.

I am a competitive, passionate, and argumentative person. Working in acutely intense environments in my twenties and into my thirties, such as running a program at summer camp or a fundraising event, I had been known to make coworkers cry with my gruff interactions, barking instructions, and arguing over the best way to do something. These characteristics were more pronounced in my youth. My hope is now, over time, growing in the Holy Spirit and fruits of the Spirit, growing in my own maturity, and submitting in discipleship, that these characteristics are less pronounced and less explosive, or at least more wisely stewarded.

I wanted to change, to take on patience, compassion, and humility. I yield to others more often, desire cooperation over competition, and take time to submit my passions to the Lord. Yes, on my worst days or when I am tired or hungry (or hangry), or when I am pushed to the edge, I am competitive and argumentative, fueled with unhinged passion, and I become like a firehose with my own agenda. But this is not who I am, it's not who I want to be, and honestly, it happens less often than before. I do not stand up and say, "This is who I am so you better deal with it, or else you are rejecting me." Growing and developing means changing. Acceptance can celebrate that growth and change.

Those who have been my friends all this time do not accept me more or less now than they did before. They did not ask me to stay stagnant. They accepted me in friendship, and also accepted, and even celebrated, as I have grown into a different person.

Gen Z and authenticity without a compass. Generation Z values authenticity, which is meant to go hand-in-hand with acceptance: *Accept me for who I am, my authentic self.* Because of this, it is important to understand what authenticity means to the next generation. To be authentic is to live life without hiding any parts of your personality or character. You are consistent in who you are. Authenticity is being the same person in all settings, public and private. In some ways, the way Gen Z uses the word *authentic* is similar to the way many older generations use the word *integrity*.

One unhealthy expression of authenticity is using it as an excuse to lack self-control. It is allowing emotions or circumstances to control our actions and interactions, rather than allowing them to exist, but also practicing self-control. This goes back to the young woman earlier who did not want to change her sarcastic interactions because "this is how I am."

Here is the rub. What if I am authentic, and you do not accept me? Do I become inauthentic to be accepted or do I remain authentic and risk rejection? Anyone who has lived through adolescence has experienced this inner tug-of-war. For today's young people, authenticity and acceptance are top generational values, but they are feeling tension when they have conflict with each other. Without a compass (like the Bible) to point in the right direction, or an anchor to their value system, Gen Z has been left with conflicting values, and no guide in how to order them. How are they supposed to figure out what to do? I can imagine the anxiety of not knowing what to do in those moments when core values are in direct opposition to each other. It would be easy to slide into a lonely place, afraid of rejection or unwilling to be honest and genuine.

Christians are exclusive. Gen Z wants to be authentic, and in their authenticity, be agreed with and not asked to change. I think you can begin to see where some of the disconnect with the church exists. This is where it gets complicated. If churches and ministries are sharing about a God who accepts all who come to him, and Gen Z is seeing a God who rejects and excludes, where is the disconnect? There is a breakdown in how these values are expressed and a disconnect in what acceptance means. The idea that God (and thus, the Christian faith) is exclusive and rejects people breaks a paramount value of this generational culture.

As previously discussed, we understand Gen Z has observed the Christian faith as exclusive, oppressive, and harmful through media and social media. This has no semblance of acceptance. We are not beginning a faith conversation with Gen Z from a neutral place; we, the church, have already been known to break their value of acceptance, and they aren't wrong, especially with their lens of what acceptance means. (Remember, we begin working within the lens of our Gen Z audience, not assuming they are working within ours.) This is not limited to how they feel about a building or an institution, but it extends to how they feel about followers of Christ like you and me. When I acknowledge I am a Christian, a Follower of Jesus, a believer, or any other descriptor, the Gen Zer before me often defaults to categorizing me as exclusive.

How does this impact evangelism and discipleship?

THE SHORT ANSWER: WILL YOU ACCEPT ME?

We are going to reword this question for our conversation around evangelism and discipleship: *Does God accept me?* God accepts all who believe in and receive Jesus, making them his own children (John 1:12). We can approach God, on his throne of grace, with confidence (Hebrews 4:16), because we are confident he will accept us and provide mercy and grace to us as his disciples. Anyone who believes in Jesus and confesses he is Lord of their lives will be accepted by God (Romans 10:9-11). God accepts those who want to offer their lives to him. We do not need to code-switch or hide parts of ourselves from God. He fully sees us. He fully knows us. He fully loves us. And that means when we ask him to take our lives, to be our hope and saving grace, he fully accepts us.

As we talk about God's acceptance with our Gen Z audience, we have to work with their generational ideas around acceptance: *Does God agree with me?* and *Will God ask me to change?* While acceptance may mean one thing to Gen Z, it is different in God's economy, and that must be explained. Jesus does not condemn the woman caught in adultery, and he also asks her to leave her life of sin (John 8:9-11). I would argue in their entire interaction we see God the Son accept her and then ask her to change. The demoniac is outcast by his people, living in a cemetery, and Jesus comes toward him and changes him (Mark 5:3-15). I would argue again that Jesus accepted this man and then changed him. Jesus invites himself to the home of Zacchaeus, and he changes his heart (Luke 19:5-8). Again, God the Son accepts Zaccheaus, and he changes him. Change is part of the promise: anyone in Christ becomes a new creation, "the old has gone, the new has come!" (2 Corinthians 5:17).

The changes mentioned here in Scripture are instantaneous changes, but there is also slower, long-term change. People like Moses and Peter changed slowly over time.

God both accepts us for who we are today and changes us at the same time. Does God accept me more now, a disciple of thirty years, than he did thirty years ago? No! We do not understand the fullness of God's acceptance in each moment of our lives, because it does not fit our picture of acceptance. It is beyond our comprehension.

But once we understand what it means to be accepted, and we understand our identity in Christ, as not only accepted in forgiveness, but made children of God, we become a good neighbor to others. As disciples, we become the hands and feet of that acceptance by God to give others a taste of God's love. As disciples of Christ, we each become a good Neighbor.

HI NEIGHBOR!

The disciple who is a Neighbor understands interconnectedness with the community and with all those who bear the image of God. The disciple who is a Neighbor understands the responsibility that comes with being a part of a community. Part of that responsibility is extending acceptance and creating belonging. A Neighbor is a neighbor not just to those who live close by, or those they like, or those who share the same faith. The outcast, downcast, marginalized, and rejected are also seen as neighbors by the Neighbor. God models acceptance to us, and we are to follow his example as we take on the feature of Neighbor as disciples of Christ. Being a Neighbor taps into Gen Z's generational values, giving them a place to express their value of acceptance in a way that glorifies God. We get to affirm the Gen Z value of acceptance and celebrate this value the Lord has built into a generation. *And* we get to offer a new way to understand and express that acceptance through being a disciple who is a Neighbor to others.

A disciple is to be a Neighbor to all people, even people they see as enemies: "You have heard that it was said, 'Love your neighbor and hate your enemy.' But I tell you, love your enemies and pray for those who persecute you" (Matthew 5:43-44). Accepting our neighbors does not mean we have to agree with them. It means seeing them through the eyes of the Lord. Accepting others is seeing them as created in God's image, as ones God desires to redeem and restore, as ones with purpose. Many times, it is setting aside what I think is comfortable to help my Neighbor feel belonging.

Being a Neighbor is loving others, which is a form of acceptance. Love facilitates and cultivates belonging. Love is more powerful than acceptance. It makes a way for acceptance. Love does not require agreement, and love can make us want to change for the better. Jesus instructs us to love our neighbors in the same way we love ourselves (Matthew 5:43-44; 19:19; 22:39; Mark 12:31, 33; Luke 10:27).

JESUS AS NEIGHBOR

I looked up the word *acceptance* in the concordance in the back of my Bible. It did not offer anything related to God accepting me. I put myself in the shoes of a Gen Zer searching for answers (though they may search TikTok before cracking the concordance), and realized how much we can help Gen Z by showing them God's acceptance in the Bible. We can point out where we see what it means to be a Neighbor.

The good Samaritan (Luke 10:25-37). Jesus is asked, "Who is my neighbor?" by an expert in the law (Luke 10:29). Jesus' story demonstrates that being a Neighbor is active. The robbed and beaten man was the neighbor of all the men in the story, but it was the Samaritan who acted as Neighbor, while a priest and Levite pass by. A Samaritan! The priest and Levite would have known the law well, been committed to a righteous way of living, and devoted to the Lord. Yet, it was the Samaritan, the despised and lower class, religiously impure, and an ethnic outsider, who Jesus uses to illustrate how to be a Neighbor.

We don't know the exact reasons the priest and Levite passed by and did not help. Maybe the priest and Levite were afraid for their own safety, or perhaps they presumed the man dead and did not want to risk becoming "unclean" by touching a dead body (see Numbers 19:11). Both are self-protective modes: *I don't want to get robbed too*, and *I don't want to become "unclean."* The latter could even be motivated by reverence for God's Law. This is a good place to pause and ask, "Have you seen places where this happens today? Do you have examples of when people have put what they think is following God's Law in front of being a Neighbor?" It's a spicy question, an uncomfortable one, but asking it gives space and permission for our Gen Z friends to ask even more questions.

Jesus has a pattern of correcting the religious teachers and experts in the law, trying to focus them on the heart of the law: "Love the Lord your God" and "Love your neighbor as yourself" (Luke 10:26-27). The heart of the law should have motivated the priest and the Levite to help the robbed and beaten man, or at least check and see if he was alive. Jesus tells us not to let the letter of the law get in the way of living out the heart of the law. Who is my neighbor? According to this passage, it is those who need mercy (Luke 10:37).

Rich, young ruler (Mark 10:17-27). A man runs up to Jesus and asks what he must do to have eternal life, as if this rich, young man is asking God, "What must I do for you to accept me?" Jesus goes on to list the commandments, something the rich, young man agrees with, and claims to have followed since he was young. This young man is concerned with the letter of the law but not the heart of it. I also think he is not being truthful. Okay, I think he is flat-out lying about his religiously obedient life. It is an impossible feat to do what the rich, young man is claiming to have done.

In the next verse, Jesus reflects God's acceptance and acts as a Neighbor. Jesus looks at the inauthentic and insecure man and loves him (Mark 10:21). Jesus loves him, just as he is, standing before God the Son. Jesus loves him, not for the things the rich, young man has done or hasn't done, but just because he's God. As we sit with this passage next to our Gen Z friends, pause here. Let's invite them to wonder what it would be like for them if they realized how much God loves them. What would be different? Stop and set a timer for simply two minutes. For those two minutes, let's sit next to our Gen Z friends, and silently focus on letting ourselves be loved. Maybe we can work our way to five minutes, or even ten, if we do this more often. This is the kind of love we get to share with our neighbors. What prevents us from experiencing God's love?

Jesus then asks this man to change: to sell everything, give it to the poor, and come follow him. This does not mean Jesus would love him more if the young man did these things. Jesus is pointing the young man back to the heart of the law: to love God and love your neighbors. Jesus asks the young man to change, to let go of what prevents him from experiencing the fullness of his love as a new creation in Christ. Jesus does not reject the young man, but in the end of this story, it seems the young man rejects Jesus.

Because Jesus is God, he fully sees and knows this rich, young man. He would have known his life up to this point, and the choice he was going to make. In the midst of that, Jesus loved him. That love is the kind of love that should be shown by a disciple who is a Neighbor. It is seeing someone in the midst of their story and struggle and showing them love. That love shows that, if you come to Christ, he will accept you.

A TALK WITH GEN Z

Being a Neighbor reminds a lonely generation they are a part of a community. Within that community of beloved ones of Christ, they now can extend the acceptance of that community to others! They can share the good news for all people who believe. Gen Z will be able to see those who have been overlooked but desperately need the gospel

I am so grateful for Generation Z and their eyes and hearts for others. Their value of acceptance is a gift to this world and a gift to the church. Gen Z pushes our older generations to wrestle with the letter of the law and the heart of the law. In discipleship, we get to work together to figure out how to be a Neighbor, each generation helping another. We can thank them for their partnership in this.

Part of this is learning how to separate acceptance and agreement. This takes time and proximity, and even verbalization.

Our Gen Z friends need to hear us say, "I may not agree with that person's view or choice, but I welcome and accept them as my neighbor," and then witness how we continue to love. Model it and allow our younger generation to see what it looks like. This is not being inauthentic, pretending to accept someone when I don't agree and want them to change. It is authentically showing love and acceptance through the Lord. Gen Z will learn from us how to extend acceptance to our neighbors as Jesus did. He accepted people as they were when they came to him, and he also changed them.

This may be a new place for our Gen Zers to step into. It is asking them to redefine the parameters of what acceptance means, reforming or breaking with how their generational culture has defined acceptance. This requires patience and courage, and partnership with a mentor, who can walk alongside and process this with a younger person, through all the different opportunities to be a Neighbor.

Gen Z's value of acceptance in the hands of the Lord will change our communities and our world. As Gen Z disciples of Christ understand what it means to be Neighbor, they can create the belonging and sense of community many are looking for. If we are willing to be uncomfortable and stretched—both as older generations allow Gen Z to live into their value of acceptance, and as Gen Z is willing to let acceptance be redefined through God's ways by being discipled by older generations—our communities will be formed into something new and life-changing.

KEY IDEAS

Ask Gen Z: What does it look like to be accepted? Where have you seen people put God's law in front of being a Neighbor? What would it be like if you realized how much God loved you? What prevents you from experiencing that?

Gen Z Asks: Will you accept me? (Will God accept me?)

Answer: God accepts all who want to follow him. He fully sees you, and knows you, and welcomes you. God both fully accepts you today when you go to him, and he also makes you into something new.

Result: As we are fully accepted into God's family, each of us learns to become a Neighbor to others: to reflect God's acceptance to others. We learn to love our neighbors as we love ourselves. This is community-changing and community-forming loving acceptance.

5

DO ALL PEOPLE MATTER TO GOD?

My friend Jeff ordered pizza to feed a group of guys doing some yard work as a fundraiser for summer camp. Because Jeff knows high school guys can eat a lot of pizza, he ordered a lot of pizza. He actually ordered too much pizza, and there was quite a bit of leftovers. The guys asked if they could pack up the leftover pizza, and of course, Jeff agreed. These high school students packed up the pizza in smaller, individual portions, and they did something Jeff had never seen before.

The guys got into their cars and drove to a part of town known to have people living on the street. Any time Jeff had seen kids give food to people in need on the street, it was because they were right there, visible and close. But these kids went out of their way and drove about twenty minutes to give their food away. You see, the people they wanted to serve were not right next to where they were doing yard work. It wasn't out of sight, out of mind. They had to make an effort, and they were willing, not only to not waste the pizza, but to help those who are in need. For these guys, it wasn't just about having enough to eat themselves; it was about feeding others also.

Remember the disciples in the boat during a storm, finding Jesus asleep in the stern (Mark 4:36-38)? Scared for their lives, the disciples wake up Jesus and ask, "Teacher, don't you care if *we* drown?" Now, each disciple did not shake Jesus and individually ask, "Don't you care if *I* drown?" It's hard for me to admit, but I think I would find comfort knowing I was not going to drown, even if others might drown. I just want to know I will be okay. I wish this wasn't true, and that I was a little more selfless or even heroic. But I'm afraid the ugly truth is that I care about me. I would ask, "Does God care about *me*?"

When it comes to God, Gen Z not only cares about *me,* but they also care about *we*: "Don't you care if *we* drown?" This generation does not want to profit when others are losing out. Gen Z especially doesn't want to profit from others' suffering. They do not want to be part of a problematic and oppressive system that results in only the survival of the fittest (or most powerful or most privileged). Does everyone in the boat matter to God? Do you care if all of us drown, not just me?

How beautiful! Many have mislabeled Gen Z as selfish or entitled. For a generation that has grown up navigating an increasingly individualistic society, there is a collectivist lens that still exists! They have seen the disproportionate dispersal of privilege and the abuse of power, and do not want to benefit if it means taking from others. They do not shrug their shoulders and accept this is the way the world is. Justice, dignity, and the care of others matters to Gen Z. Gen Z wants to know: *Do all people matter to God?*

A WALK WITH GEN Z

In 2020, Gen Z ranged from ages 8 to 23, which means most of Gen Z was in the midst of adolescence when the Covid-19 closures took place. At a critical point of their development, they were moved from classrooms and clubs to isolation. Many aspects of social development moved from in-person to a screen. It boosted the influence of digital and social media in the lives of adolescents, even more so with the lack of in-person social interaction. There were hundreds and thousands of voices coming at them through social media—a constant, insurmountable influx of information invading Gen Z in the digital space.

Social justice found Gen Z. Gen Z was also in the midst of adolescence when social justice issues were at the forefront of conversations in media and digital media. Health care, unemployment, and food insecurity were widely discussed as a result of the 2020 closures, highlighting the needs of the most vulnerable. The deaths of George Floyd and Breonna Taylor in the spring of 2020 were very visible for Gen Z, shared widely through social media, sparking social justice demonstrations and public cries for police reform. This generation was surrounded by social justice conversations in their digital world, where they spent hours each day. Whether or not they were looking for the conversation, it was looking for them. Whatever they experienced, believed, or valued, conversations around social justice were shoved in front of them and demanded some kind of engagement.

Gen Z learned very quickly how to participate in social issues through the vehicle of social media. One example of this was the movement to post a black square on social media platforms, such as Instagram, during Blackout Tuesday (June 2, 2020). The purpose was to bring attention to and mourn racial injustice, protest police brutality, and fight for changes in racist or racially biased policy. This was paired with using hashtags like #BLM or #BlackLivesMatter. Additional hashtags entered the social media space like #icantbreathe to recall George Floyd's repeated words under the knee of police officer Derek Chauvin and #sayhername to remember the wrongful death of Breonna Taylor. Gen Z was using their digital world to interact with real-world issues and learning to practice digital advocacy for their real-world principles.

At the same time, Gen Z also learned the pitfalls of popularized digital advocacy. Blackout Tuesday was not an action Gen Z could opt into to advocate for change; it became a sociocultural requirement. For many Gen Zers, a decision was required on whether or not to post a black square in their social accounts to show their support for the Black community. Still, *not* posting a black square communicated a message, whether intentionally or unintentionally, of indifference to racial injustice or opposition to change. To complicate factors, there were also those who supported the Black community and anti-racist policy but did not support the Black Lives Matter organization itself due to its organizational values. What were they supposed to do?

If that wasn't confusing enough, the cultural tide suddenly shifted in the digital space. By the end of the day on Blackout Tuesday, headlines began to emerge that posting a black box was doing more harm than good.[1] A search for Black Lives Matter on Instagram would result in numerous posts of black boxes rather than informational posts. The days that followed brought backlash and criticism to those who participated in the social media campaign. Those who just days before were applauded for their social justice advocacy were now being slammed in social media circles (and in real life) for being shallow, ineffective, and even lazy (*Am I enough?*).[2] There were new instructions and suggestions for how to advocate for change circulating social and digital media.

Most of this took place in a digital setting, but it had real-world social, relational, and political consequences. Many adults from previous generations were blind to the pressure Gen Z adolescents faced to do and say the correct thing, or risk falling outside their generation's social justice values. Again, most of Gen Z were adolescents during this time, and these digital social justice movements spoke into the formation of their values in a key window of development. Most adults did not understand the space our young people inhabited.

Social justice and the church. Does Gen Z wonder whether God cares about social justice, or if God is actually the source of injustice (*Is God good?*), or if Christians misunderstanding or misrepresenting God are the problem? I recommend we go straight to the source. It is a worthy question to ask. Even if we think we know the answer, asking the question honors the person in front of you.

Take a moment to ask a Gen Zer, "Does God care about social justice?" Give them space to share what they think or believe, and listen for the purpose of understanding, not correcting. Recall that Gen Z views Christians as ignorant, uninformed, hypocritical, irrelevant, and judgmental. All these descriptors are obstacles to the idea that social justice has been part of the Christian faith. Actually, all of these descriptive words would be used to describe those who are part of the injustice problem. Thus, Gen Z does not generally trust Christians, and, as a result, the Christian faith, and possibly God (*Can I trust you?*).

Part of the reason for this is that Gen Z has grown up in a time where media attention has been focused on various corruptions, atrocities, and abuses committed by or within the church. They have watched television shows or series, movies, and social media depicting how Christians are responsible for systemic injustices. Gen Z's experience with the Christian faith has been in seeing colonization and cultural assimilation mixed with evangelism. Gen Z has seen the stories told in social media, television, and movies of Native peoples who were separated from their families and sent to religious residential schools, stripped of their cultural identity, and suffered abuses at the hands of Christian missionaries. Testimonies of physical and sexual abuse by Christian leaders, and the accompanying religious trauma, are shared throughout the digital space, including streaming services like Netflix. This younger generation is aware of how the Bible was used to defend social injustices like slavery, racism, sexism, and more. It is hard to stomach this.

I came across a celebrity sharing about his faith on Instagram. Of course, I sprinted to the comments and almost immediately read a comment referring to Christianity as "one of the most repressive establishments in the world," which continued, "How many people are prosecuted and can't be free because of Christianism?" The comment finished with a rejection of the Christian faith because the atrocities done in the name of God cannot be forgotten. At that point, this comment had garnered over three hundred likes. It resonates with the understanding of Christianity Gen Z has been surrounded by.

I did not realize how this impacted Gen Z until I was talking to a high school junior, who told me she had refused to come to anything "religious" because of "how Christians are depicted in the media." All of this, and much more dialogue in social media spaces on the injustices carried out by Christians, has contributed to an atmosphere of distrust of the Christian faith, seeing it as a corrupt, abusive, colonizing, and harmful belief system. It is no wonder the next generation sees Christians as harmful, intolerant, or oppressive. With this information, why would a generation, or anyone, want anything to do with God or Christianity?

This is the atmosphere Jude 3 Project entered, to help Christians, especially those of African descent, understand the Chrisitan faith, church history, and their reasons for believing. They tackle the social justice–minded questions being asked in our current cultural moment: Is Christianity homophobic? Is Christianity a White man's religion? Does Christianity oppress women?[3] These questions are not limited to the Black community. They are being asked widely by a generation who cares about social justice and does not trust that the Christian faith or Christian God reflects those values. *Do all people matter to God?*

With this understanding of church history and Christianity, many do not see how God the Father, Jesus the Son, and the Holy Spirit have actually formed many, if not all of the social justice values this generation holds so tightly to. From their lens, Gen Z sees how their values stand against the Christian faith, not with it. Gen Z does not witness the church taking an active role in social justice issues, or at least the issues that matter to them.

This has also impacted the Black Christian youth community, which is often associated with social activism. Almeda M. Wright outlines the lack of connection between personal spirituality and activism for young African Americans, noting that African American Christian youth "are being taught that their faith should *only* address their personal or spiritual lives."[4] Charles E. Goodman Jr. of Tabernacle Baptist Church calls for Black churches to return to collectivist activism, citing critics who say the issues facing the Black community are not addressed by the Black church. This has contributed to a disconnect between spiritual lives and real-life experiences, which could and should be tied together in communal activism.[5] Goodman explains, "The shift towards individualism has engendered a diminution of the communal spirit that once defined the Black church and possibly a reduction in its engagement in community activism."[6]

To Gen Z, social awareness and advocacy is, at best, a dormant aspect of the Christian faith and, at worst, was always absent from the church. Because of this, they are unaware that many of the ethics they hold and are fighting for are rooted in Christian ethics. Charity, education, medical care, and hospitals all have roots in Christianity.

THE SHORT ANSWER: DO ALL PEOPLE MATTER TO GOD?

God created all humans with the imago Dei, the image of God (Genesis 1:26-27). This is the reason murder is a big deal to God: "For in the image of God has / God made mankind" (Genesis 9:6). Being made in the image of God is what makes every person worthy of dignity, care, and knowing the love of Christ. The image of God cannot be removed from any human being, and God cares about every person.

In the Gospel of Luke, Jesus shares the Sermon on the Plain (Luke 6:17-49). It strips away the spiritual language from the Beatitudes in the Sermon on the Mount (Matthew 5:3-12) and allows the concrete needs of his audience to stand out:

Blessed are you who are poor. (Luke 6:20)

Blessed are you who hunger now. (Luke 6:21)

Blessed are you who weep now. (Luke 6:21)

Blessed are you when people hate you, when they exclude and insult you and reject your name as evil. (Luke 6:22)

In his own words, God expresses his care for the poor, the hungry, the mourning, the hated, the outcast, the insulted, and the rejected. More notably included in the Sermon on the Plain are woes: woe to those who are rich, who are well fed, who laugh, and who everyone speaks well of (Luke 6:24-26). God reverses and reorders societal power structures and values and gives a frame of reference for disciples as Prophets.

Jesus also ministered to those in power, those who stole from others, and to a religious insider, a Pharisee named Nicodemus. Jesus' actions reflect a desire for people, from all walks of life, who have done all kinds of things, to be redeemed and restored: for God so loved the world (John 3:16), and all who are in it. Jesus came to offer freedom and make a new way.

God not only sees the poor, the marginalized, the outcast, the rejected, and the suffering, but he also knows these experiences personally. Jesus, God the Son, was born in a stable because there was not enough housing for his family. Early in his life, he was a refugee in Egypt, displaced from his home. He called social, religious, and ethnic outsiders to follow him, and he suffered a criminal's death. Jesus did not arrive as an earthly king with power, privilege, and possession, but walked the walk of the very people we are asking God if he cares about.

God's love is active and reflects the kingdom of heaven here on earth. God's love moves us to use what we have to feed the hungry, give drink to the thirsty, clothe the naked, and care for the sick (Matthew 25:34-40). God's love calls us to fight against injustice and simultaneously pray for the redemption and restoration of our enemy.

Prophet and Steward are two features of a disciple that reflect the values of Gen Z and reflect the kingdom of heaven here on earth.

SEE, SAY, AND DO

There are two features of a disciple to pair with Gen Z's value for social justice and the question *Do all people matter to God?* First, we will look at being a Prophet as a disciple. Cahalan describes a Prophet as someone who sees the social, cultural, and systemic realities that harm people.[7] A Prophet pays attention to hatred, pride, greed, disdain, and selfishness, all of which harms our neighbor.[8] A Prophet does not just notice, but also says something and calls others to action. This may be a new or different way for many of us to look at a prophetic voice: someone who notices injustice or harm, says something, and spurs action. By practicing being a Prophet, a disciple calls people to submit to God and God's ways. They represent God's truth and love in a call to action to reject the things that are unjust.

The second feature is Steward. Stewards use resources wisely to care for others. Stewards understand that they are a member of a community, which comes with responsibility to that community. A Steward does not hoard, self-protect, or ignore the needs of others. A Steward understands that all resources are God's, not any one individual's, and that the Steward is charged with how to best care for others with those resources.

JESUS AS PROPHET AND STEWARD

Jesus forms Prophets and Stewards. The Gospel of Luke reveals Jesus Christ as the Messiah, and as the Savior for all people, not only Israel.[9] Luke's Gospel answers the question *Do all people matter to God?* It announces a salvation available to all people through the Savior, no matter their pedigree, power, ethnicity, age, gender, and on and on. Salvation is accessible to all! In Luke 4:16-18, Jesus unrolls the scroll of the prophet Isaiah to declare that he has come

> to proclaim good news to the poor.
> He has sent me to proclaim freedom for the prisoners
>   and recovery of sight for the blind,
> to set the oppressed free.

Through his ministry and storytelling, Jesus demonstrates the gospel is for all kinds of people, because all people matter to God. For example, Jesus tells the story of a good Samaritan (Luke 10:25-37). The Samaritan, the undesirable character to the audience of Jesus' story, bandaged the wounds of the beaten man; carried him on his donkey; took him to a hotel; cared for him; and paid for his room, board, and care when he was gone. The Samaritan used his own time and resources to care for another in need.

Jesus gives us a call to action: "Go and do likewise" (Luke 10:37). Go and do not ignore the injustice and hurt around you. Go and use your resources to care for others. A Prophet calls others to action, and there is a call to action here by Jesus as a Prophet. A Steward shares personal resources to help others, and Jesus illustrates stewardship through the Samaritan's actions.

Zacchaeus is formed as Steward and Prophet. In Luke's Gospel account of Zacchaeus (Luke 19:1-9), we witness what happens when a person's heart is changed by Jesus. God moves a person from sinner to Steward. Zacchaeus was a chief tax collector and wealthy. As the story goes, tax collectors at the time of Jesus were infamous for making an income by skimming off the top. This was not an honest day's work—it was lying to and cheating their neighbors and community for profit. It is a good example of the misuse of power and a privileged position. After all, Zacchaeus has the weight of the Roman government behind his theft, leaving his victims powerless. Recall also that Zacchaeus is not Roman, but an Israelite. He is not only a liar and a cheat, but a betrayer of his own people, trading them for the benefits of the occupying power of Rome.

Curious about Jesus, Zacchaeus climbs up a sycamore-fig tree to see him, and when Jesus reaches that place, he calls Zacchaeus down, saying, "I must stay at your house today" (Luke 19:5). As I have shared this interaction with Jesus many times in large and small group settings of adolescents, I could have stopped at this point and pointed out to my adolescent audience, "Look! Jesus knows Zacchaeus's name and wants to spend time with him, even after all he has done!" This could have been the conclusion of my message: Jesus knows your name and wants to be with you. This is true, and it is good news, but that is not the whole story.

If we stop here, we ignore Zacchaeus's victims, those who had been cheated, lied to, and taken advantage of. Stopping here also ignores how this interaction with Jesus Christ, God the Son, changes Zacchaeus. Gen Z might be tempted to mutter about Jesus, like the people in this story did, though Gen Z's muttering might be, "He does not care about the oppressed, only the powerful. Look how he goes to the house of the one who has stolen from and taken advantage of others." Where is the justice? Does Zacchaeus simply get a pass because Jesus knows his name? Do all people matter to God, or just the rich and powerful?

The real question is, what happens to the heart of the lying, cheating betrayer when God gets a hold of it? Zacchaeus is changed by his interaction with God the Son. He now stands and says, "Here and now I give half of my possessions to the poor, and if I have cheated anybody out of anything, I will pay back four times the amount" (Luke 19:8). This is Zacchaeus becoming a Steward as a disciple of Jesus. When God gets a hold of Zacchaeus's heart, it becomes more like God's, and God's heart is both for Zaccheaus and for the poor. Zacchaeus's stewardship, his generosity to the poor, is a direct result of being changed by God, who cares about all people. God is also just and fair, and that justice is seen in Zacchaeus's decision to repay those he has cheated and then some. Again, Zacchaeus's heart is being changed to look more like God's heart. God cares about justice, and so we see Zacchaeus engage in just actions in his repentance for what he has done.

Let's be clear, Zacchaeus did not give to the poor or repay those he cheated to earn God's forgiveness (*Am I enough? Will you accept me?*). Zacchaeus did these things in response to the changing of his heart by God. His generosity is a result of becoming a Steward, caring for others with the resources at his disposal.

Zacchaeus is also embodying the disciple feature of a Prophet. Until I read this passage with eyes for Gen Z, I had never seen Zacchaeus as a Prophet, not in the traditional sense. But if the definition of a Prophet is someone who notices injustice or harm, says something, and spurs action, I see it in Zaccheaus. He notices injustice and harm by recognizing that he cheated people out of money and by seeing the existence of those in need, "the poor" (Luke 19:8). He says something. Maybe he's not calling others out, but he announces his participation in cheating, and recognizes the poor. He spurs action by changing his own personal habit, moving from taking to generosity. Do we assume no one else is changed by Zacchaeus's prophetic actions? Who else decides to help those in need because of what Zacchaeus does? Is there a hug exchanged between Zaccheaus and Matthew, who had also been a Jewish tax collector who left tax collecting behind? Are there others who do the same?

Pause and step out of a traditional idea of what a Prophet looks like, and look at Zacchaeus like he is a member of Gen Z. If a Gen Zer called attention to a population harmed and in need, owned and rectified personal contribution to the harm and need, and took new action moving forward to share and care, wouldn't we recognize the qualities of a Prophet? Zacchaeus's actions after being with Jesus also communicate that cheating others and withholding charity should be rectified. Zacchaeus recognized how he had taken advantage of people within the power systems and structures to which he had access, and Zacchaeus took action.

A TALK WITH GEN Z

After my freshman year of high school, I went to a Young Life summer camp, and I was deeply moved by the message of what was accomplished on the cross. I remember thinking, *I can't believe he did that for me!* I have heard the story of the cross often paired with this sentiment: *If you were the only person in the world, Jesus would still have died for you.* While this may be true (I generally don't like to work in theological hypotheticals), it is a mistake to focus mainly on individualized salvation when talking to Gen Z. God's restoration is more vast and awesome. While a personal nature of faith is important to Gen Z, this generation has a collective expectation of God. Gen Z is not only asking, "Does God care about me?" They are also asking, "Who else does God care about?" If God doesn't care about the outcast, oppressed, marginalized, and rejected, Gen Z does not want anything to do with the Christian God. This is a generation of prophets, and we need Generation Z.

Remember the story of Jesus calming the storm? Before the storm, the passage notes that "there were also other boats with him" (Mark 4:36). We see and hear the disciples' perspective, but what did the other boats experience? Could they see or hear Jesus from where they were, tossed by the sea in the noise of wind and waves? *Do all people matter to God?* In our study of Scripture, let's zoom out and expand the story to show our Gen Z friends that God is doing multiple things at once, both for the "main characters" of the passage, and for those in the periphery who are typically unseen. When reading or sharing the Bible, pay attention to the others in the story—the crowd, the leaders, the children—who are present, but are maybe not the focus of what is going on. Ask, Why were they there?

What was their experience? How did they experience God in this moment?

I am increasingly aware that in the Lord's justice there is a desire for restoration. It is not only Zacchaeus paying back what he stole. It is Peter becoming a rock of the Christian church after denying knowing Jesus. It is Paul becoming an apostle after murdering Christians. It is the Samaritan woman becoming the first evangelist, changing other people's lives after meeting Jesus at the well. The grace I receive is the same grace previous generations of Christ-followers have also received. The saving good news of Jesus Christ is not just for me; it is also for my neighbor, for those down the road or in the next county, for those I have hurt and for those who hurt me, for those who are both seen and unseen. It is for all people.

As we teach Gen Z to grow as Prophets and Stewards, we have to unpack what it looks like for them to do what Jesus commands: "Go and do likewise" (Luke 10:37). As we disciple Gen Z, we can ask:

1. What do you notice?
2. What do you have?
3. What can you do?

What does Gen Z notice? Where can Gen Z help the church engage with social injustices in a way that honors the heart of God? How can the church reflect God's heart for all people in action for social and systemic change? We begin by asking our Gen Z friends: What harm and injustice do you notice, little or big? Listening to Gen Z and noticing what they notice can help us live out the gospel in those foolish, radical, world-changing ways. Try to understand how Gen Z sees the world, and see where God's character is reflected in their understanding. Give Gen Z space to pause and notice.

What does Gen Z have? To help our Gen Z friends understand stewardship, we start by asking, "What do you have?" If stewardship means using what we have to help and care for others, we have to know what resources we have. It could be time, money, influence, proximity, knowledge, skill, and so much more. Help Gen Z see what they have.

After one camp gathering, a young man approached me and said, "I think I'm supposed to be a Steward, but I don't know where to start." I asked him what he was involved with at school. "I run track," he responded. That is what he had. I said to him,

> What if you gave your track season to God? Tell God this track season is for him, not you. Ask God to show you how he can use you to help others. Maybe it is giving a word of encouragement to an athlete or coach. Maybe it is offering to pray for a teammate before a race. Maybe it is putting equipment away when you don't have to. Your area of influence is the track team. Ask God how you can use what you have to help and care for others.

Our work is to provide concrete ways to express the disciple features of Prophet and Steward. We have to get out of the habit of our sermons, lessons, and studies centering almost exclusively on spiritual responses, and increasingly include social, communal, and practical applications. We have to answer the question of how following Jesus impacts our relationship with money, time, influence, and so on, in everyday life. God is not only in the business of changing our personal lives, but our communities also. Our Gen Z friends don't need more of anything to help others, but they do need help seeing what they have and how it can be used.

What can Gen Z do? Wisdom needs to be paired with Prophecy and Stewardship. Stewards will probably not have enough to care for all the needs they come across. Prophets notice a lot—and Gen Z is especially attuned to the injustice and harm taking place in the world, but we have not generally taught Gen Z what to do with that. Wisdom helps us understand what to do, cultivating the spiritual skill of listening to the Holy Spirit for direction.

Talk to Gen Z about that gut feeling, or when they feel their blood pressure rise and heart rate increase. We can share with our Gen Z friends that these could be signals to go to the Lord in prayer. Ask him to separate our own bias, lens, and sin from what we notice so that we can better pay attention to what God is wanting to show us or tell us. None of us are immune from mishearing or misunderstanding the Holy Spirit.

To act as Prophets and Stewards without first seeking the wisdom of the Lord is a mistake. There is wisdom in listening to the Lord. Our Gen Z friends all know someone who constantly complains or criticizes, who has become like a "resounding gong or a clanging cymbal" because it seemed there was no love behind their words (1 Corinthians 13:1). Their words lose meaning and so their message is ignored. Wisdom can mean knowing how and when to say something in love, not in hate or disdain. All people matter to God, and this is where the skill and wisdom of speaking truth in love is an important part of discipleship.

Provide places for our Gen Zer to practice *doing*. At our weekly Bible study, I asked a group of high school students, "What have you learned about money?" Immediately, they talked about saving for retirement. Then I asked, "What have you learned about giving money?" There was a pause, some blank looks, and then one student piped up, "You have to be careful about who you give to because a lot of times, that money can go to administrative costs and not to actually help people." And that was it. No one had taught them how to give.

We began a month-long journey of discussing how to steward through giving. It culminated with pooling some money together (most of it came from me). I asked each student to present an organization they believed in to discuss with our group. They brought a range of different nonprofits, from a club at their high school that helped kids in the band get instruments they couldn't afford, to an environmental cause, to a charity that helped displaced women and children. They each shared, and then we voted together on where the money should go. We even discussed whether all the money should go to one spot, or if a percentage of the money should go to different places based on the number of votes it got. We practiced being Prophets and Stewards by noticing needs, and then using what we had to help.

We can't assume someone else is teaching these skills. They aren't being passed down. It is our responsibility to open the conversation, and not to assume someone else already has. Don't just talk about resources theoretically; provide real-life practice. Show Gen Z how to do it.

The features of Prophet and Steward are exercised directly in community with others. They are tied to being a Neighbor and Forgiver. As Gen Z grows into living out these features of a disciple, they will change our churches, our communities, and our world, showing us how to live, serve, and love in community in ways we have not known before.

KEY IDEAS

Ask Gen Z: Does God care about social justice? What do you notice? What do you have? What can you do with what you notice and what you have?

Gen Z Asks: Do all people matter to God?

Response: God cares about the restoration and redemption of all people. The ministry of Jesus continually reflects love in action for the poor, the hungry, the outcast, the rejected, and the marginalized.

Result: Being a Prophet and Steward allows Gen Z to engage their generational value of social justice (and acceptance) and reflect the heart of God within this world. This engages with our community and caring for our neighbor.

6

CAN I TRUST YOU?

Some of my favorite research to do is simply listening to the Gen Zers around me. I texted some Gen Z young women this question: "How do you know if you can trust someone?" Here are some of their responses:

- "I feel like I can really trust someone when we're really close or I've known them for a long time. They really see me and know me and prove they are trustworthy."
- "I see how they act with other people, like if they gossip, and see if they have good friendships. If they don't have good friendships, it might be because they aren't trustworthy."
- "I have to understand and know someone first to know if they are trustworthy."
- "If I know they really, truly care about me."
- "If someone keeps their promises, is honest, or kind, then over time and with experiences, I know I can trust that person."

These responses are filled with wisdom and discernment, and I noticed trust was not immediately given. No one said they trust first until that trust is broken. Each response reflected a patient, wait-and-see approach. They take time to discover if a person is trustworthy or not. Gen Z is slow to give their trust away. They highly value trust, and they are not looking to squander it.

I often hear trust spoken about as a holistic quality. Either someone is trustworthy, or not. The question of trust is related to the questions of acceptance, enoughness, safety, and goodness:

- Can I trust you will accept me? If you do not accept me, I cannot trust you.
- Can I trust you will not reject me? If I am not enough for you to love and value me, I cannot trust you.
- Can I trust I will be safe with you? If you compromise my safety, I cannot trust you.
- Can I trust you are good? If you are not, I cannot trust you.

Trust is built through time and experiences like being seen and known, being accepted and loved, and feeling safe. Trust is more easily built with those who share common experiences because there is a shared understanding and less to explain, facilitating a feeling of being seen and known.

We are not entitled to be trusted by Gen Z. They are keen observers of character. Of course, they make mistakes and trust the wrong people, as we all do. They are still developing their compasses. Still, I don't take their trust for granted. To be trusted by a Gen Zer is an honor.

A WALK WITH GEN Z

Gen Z has grown up with endless information pursuing them on multiple platforms through the devices in their hands.

Their brains learned how to quickly sort and sift the immeasurable amount of media they consume.[1] Gen Z has had to figure out who to trust in a split second. If you watch Gen Zers maneuver their phones, they move at lightspeed. Each video, post, story, and episode they see is moving through this filter: *Can I trust you?*

Playing hide-and-seek. One of the dynamics born out of growing up with smartphones, social media, and digital media is that Gen Z is aware that a person can have different personalities in different spaces. I guess this has always been true in some sense. A person can be one way publicly and different behind closed doors, but now we can view it online. The honest presentation of who one is in all settings and circumstances, in public and in private, is part of the criteria for trust. To be described as authentic is to be worthy of trust.

Gen Z's identity formation was not limited to their physical world (what can be seen or touched), or what was nearby. They were given an easy and accessible way to be a different person online than in real life. Anyone can be one way in real life and different ways on different accounts and platforms. A hobby, a part of a personality, and even a character someone can play all find room to grow and develop in virtual spaces, while remaining hidden in the real world. One survey, conducted by tech company Lenovo, found that 68 percent of Gen Zers who responded felt a disconnect between who they were online and who they were in real life, leading to feelings of anxiety, depression, and loneliness.[2] In other words, the lack of integrated identity contributes to poor mental health.

This phenomenon has been described as the development of hybrid or dual identities, or avatars.[3] These develop from having both virtual lives and in-person lives. Identities can remain fragmented from each other because they have distinct, separate spaces to exist. The lack of integration of these different parts of one's personality can continue for prolonged amounts of time, as this digitally savvy generation has figured out how to preserve a digital identity in private or separate spaces.

This may sound crazy to a member of the older generations who either never have existed in the virtual space or were introduced as adults. Gen Z existed in the virtual space during adolescence, when identity formation was doing the bulk of its work. Fragmented identities are not foreign or strange to Gen Z. They are used to people having different identities, personalities, and even morals in different spaces.

OnlyFans is an app where subscribers pay to stream video content from specific users. The app is advertised as sharing subscriptions to host accounts for multiple genres of interest like cooking, fitness, or music, though OnlyFans is primarily known for and associated with sharing explicit content. Whether or not Gen Z is engaged with the app, its existence and reputation are well known by Gen Z. They're aware of news stories reporting teachers fired for what they shared on OnlyFans.[4] It is more proof to Gen Z that any of us can present ourselves as an upstanding, principled mentor, but may also have an OnlyFans account, expressing very different values than we present.

Gen Z knows anyone can hide anything. They are acutely aware of how easy it is to be a different person in different virtual spaces, and they do not assume we are who we say we are all the time. Gen Z is constantly analyzing those around them, wondering, *Can I trust you? Are you who you say you are all the time? What are you hiding?*

Spam. One of my Gen Z friends told me, "I'm going to invite you to my spam account." I already followed her on Instagram, but she revealed to me the account I followed was a filtered account. Only certain things were posted there. Her spam account was more unfiltered, and only her trusted friends were invited to follow that account. There, she could post without risk of embarrassment or judgment because she had curated her audience. She could be authentic there. She decided I was trustworthy enough to see that side of her, the side only shared with a select group.

In 2022, a smartphone app called BeReal gained popularity with young people. The name of the app confronted the inauthenticity in the social media world, challenging users to *be real.* The concept was simple: instead of only cultivating and sharing photos that make your life seem glamorous, exciting, or worthy of envy, post reality by honestly sharing whatever you are doing at a particular time chosen by the app.

An alarm went off for all users on the BeReal app at a different time each day. Users had two minutes to take and post a photo of where they were and what they were doing at that very moment. Users were supposed to use the first photo taken, unlike choosing the best photo from multiple tries (the app shared if multiple photos were taken before posting). BeReal was designed to be an honest sharing of everyday life, capturing not only the exciting and glamorous, but the boring and common: lying in bed, doing chores, working on homework, or doing nothing. This app appealed to Gen Z's longing for real and authentic content. It was a chance to see what people were really doing.

It didn't take much time for digitally savvy app users to figure out how to work around the strict guidelines for authenticity. BeReal allowed people to post outside the two-minute window and simply timestamped the photo to notify followers of the tardy post. In my conversations with Gen Zers, they had become less concerned with sharing authentically on time, and more concerned with sharing what they preferred to share at a different time. This produced a different outcome than the app was designed for, as users concluded, *If everyone wasn't going to be honest, why should I?* The app designed to offer an authentic space, especially for Gen Z, was now becoming a less-trustworthy platform.

Two years after the app gained popularity, I was sitting in a room of people when the familiar BeReal timer went off on a person's phone. Another person commented in a dismissive tone, "Do people still use that?" The less authentic, honest, and trustworthy the app became, the more Gen Z began to abandon it: *I cannot trust you.*

"Facts" and TikTok. In my lifetime, I have gone from seeing the news on four broadcast channels, to twenty-four–hour news outlets on cable TV, to online newspapers and news channels, and all the way to smartphone apps and news through social media. The news market is saturated. With so many options to view the news, each platform is vying for our attention and targeting an audience, so much so that now certain news outlets are associated with particular social, political, and even religious views. This skews the news as it is reported through a specific lens that is attractive to the audience.

Gen Z is aware of this and is not quick to trust information shared in the media. They see news and media outlets tied to power and institutions who have agendas. Because information coming out of those outlets has agendas tied to it, it may not be completely trustworthy.

Gen Z is also aware that for every "fact" or piece of information shared in the media, they can go online and find opposing "facts" and information. They can pull up their phone and disprove statements using the endless information available to them. Access to smartphones, the internet, and social media means Gen Z can find multiple views on any given topic. I get fact-checked regularly as I talk with Gen Zers.

As digital natives, Gen Z is aware they are surrounded by false, altered, or biased media, images, and information. It is common to take many photos of a particular moment to choose the best one to share and post. That spontaneous, candid moment shared is not so candid. Gen Z has photo-editing software at their fingertips, and recognizes poorly edited photos. This was at the center of the "Where is Kate Middleton?" phenomenon. People scoured a Mother's Day photo of Princess Kate with her children shared with the media and discussed the alterations and edits, proving it was not evidence the "missing" Princess Kate was okay (and this contributed to increased distrust of an institution). Kate Middleton was indeed not okay, and it was revealed she was privately fighting cancer. AI-generated photos from the 2024 Met Gala circulated on social media. They depicted two celebrities who did not actually attend, Rihanna and Katy Perry, and the photos fooled many. Seeing is not necessarily believing.

We have gone from seeing current events caught by one video camera, to multiple smartphones by eyewitnesses providing different angles and perspectives. In 2023, adolescents rated TikTok as the most authentic media compared to traditional media, streaming services, and video games.[5] Still, Gen Z will say TikTok is fake, toxic, and unreliable.

Pause and think about what this means. Gen Z's most authentic media is still widely unreliable. Gen Z is not necessarily saying TikTok is a good source of information. They are saying all media is so untrustworthy that even the most "authentic" media is full of false information. It is the least of all evils, but still pretty evil. Gen Z is saying, *I cannot trust any media.*

Streamed and exposed. Gen Z is aware of the misuse of power and authority by people and institutions in the world. Stories from the past are being told from new perspectives. It seems like a new documentary is constantly popping up on streaming services promising shock, intrigue, and new perspectives on events or well-known figures like *Britney vs. Spears* (2021), *Jimmy Savile: A British Horror Story* (2022), and the *Untold* series of documentaries on Netflix. There are documentaries focused on scandals in religious institutions like *Shiny Happy People* (2023), *The Secrets of Hillsong* (2023), and *Dancing for the Devil: The 7M TikTok Cult* (2024).

Through exposés, testimonies on social media, and Netflix documentaries, we have seen the dark side of what were thought to be good and trustworthy people and organizations. More and more, Gen Z has been exposed to the misuse of authority and power to take advantage of and harm others.

Because it often takes years to acquire title, responsibility, authority, or power, those at the top of the leadership pyramid tend to be those of previous generations. Maybe in the past, someone in a position of power or authority automatically was granted our trust. Previous generations may have concluded this person had proved themselves trustworthy in order to be where they are. Gen Z knows this is not necessarily true. "Respect your elders" used to be a cultural norm. Gen Z does

not assume respect is deserved with the accumulation of
years, and has a general distrust of parents, elders, experts,
and other authority figures, keeping an eye out for symptoms
of hypocrisy.[6]

Cancel culture has contributed to a context of distrust, both
in the existence of cancel culture and what we are watching
happen through cancel culture. It seems to thrive on aiming its
target at people who had reputations for being noble, upright,
and admirable, and proving otherwise: *You thought this person
was one way, but it turns out they are the opposite.* The longer
period of time that passes before something is discovered and
exposed, the longer road of trust that was built, and the bigger
hurt inflicted.

For Gen Z, the higher the power distance, position distance,
and even age distance, the lower the trust. We do not earn
Gen Z's trust with a title or authority. It is quite the opposite.
We have to prove we are trustworthy despite those things. This
means many of us must recognize we are starting with a dis-
advantage when we meet a Gen Zer.

I have served in ministry to adolescents for over twenty-five
years. I am now the same age as the parents of the students
I serve. When Gen Zers meet me, they are not culturally dis-
posed to trust me because of my age, experience, education,
length of time following the Lord, knowledge of Scripture,
or job title. Instead, Gen Z may assume I am hypocritical, irrelevant, harmful, bigoted, and inauthentic.

Church hurts. In a 2024 interview, Kara Powell discussed
the need to rebuild or build trust with younger generations:
"[Gen Z and Alpha have] lost trust with institutions. They have
lost trust with adults. They have lost trust with church, and I

mean church including faith community in general, and sadly we in the faith community, we have earned that lack of trust."[7]

Gen Z generally does not trust religion or religious institutions. In a 2023 study by Springtide Research Institute, only 28 percent of those aged 13–25 have a high level of trust in organized religion.[8] They recognize the impact of the sins of the church, from the Crusades to the Spanish Inquisition, from Manifest Destiny to covered-up sexual abuse, and more, leading Gen Z to view Christians as harmful. I went onto Instagram and searched the hashtags #churchabuse and #churchtrauma, and thousands of posts came up. From the stories of sexual abuse and cover-ups, the abuse of children, and leaders profiting from financial contributions intended to help others, there is story after story of how the church has hurt people, especially children.

This leads to a distrust in God. *Can I trust you?* is extended to *Can I trust God?* If God's so-called representatives are untrustworthy, is the same true for God? If the Bible has been used to perpetuate harmful actions and institutions (like slavery), can Gen Z trust the Bible?

I garner distrust from Gen Z because of my age, position, and authority. This distrust doubles down when they find out I am a Follower of Jesus. This is quite different from when I grew up. I have to practice seeing this through the lens of Gen Z, not my own lens. I am entering into their world, asking for their trust, and so their lens is to be used. Gen Z has had plenty of reasons not to easily trust others, and it trickles down to personal relationships.

Distrust trickle-down effect. In my conversations with Gen Z, I find they are generally less likely to believe people are "basically good" than previous generations. Even friends do not trust the nice things they hear from their friends. One college student told me, "My friends might say something nice about me, like a compliment, but in my head, I think, they don't mean that." I pressed in to inquire why he thought this. Shouldn't we trust what our friends say about us? "People just say things," he said, "You never know what is real or not, and no one wants to offend anyone else by telling the truth. So, it's easier to lie just to make people feel better and not offend them." In other words, everyone lies to protect each other's feelings, even friends, so Gen Z concludes, *When others say something nice to me, they are probably lying too.*

I was saddened by his words. Imagine coming of age, not knowing if you could even trust the nice things your friends say. I also thought, *What does this mean for my interactions with Gen Z?* How many times will I not only have to repeat the affirmations and encouragements I give but somehow also demonstrate those affirmations and encouragements through action? Gen Zers will not believe us when we say something good about who they are. We will have to repeat it over and over, and demonstrate it, until our Gen Z friends pause and say, "You really mean that, don't you?"

I have to remind myself that it takes more time to build relationships with Gen Z. Anyone working with Gen Z needs to be given the time and space necessary to cultivate close relationships and belonging with our Gen Z friends—more time and space than many realize. Trusting relationships cannot be rushed into fast-paced strategies, flashy programs, and growth plans. Go slow. Be patient. Walk closely. We have to earn trust through a collection of experiences over a length of time.

Gen Z is aware they are surrounded by lies, a context that creates questions about who they can trust—including the question *Can I trust God?*

THE SHORT ANSWER: CAN I TRUST YOU?

Gen Z is dealing with doubt in God—doubt in who God is, and doubt in his trustworthiness. Let's go back to the intertwined questions posed at the start of the chapter, as if they are statements from Gen Z to God:

- If God does not accept me (according to the Gen Z understanding of acceptance), I cannot trust God.

- If I am not enough for God to love and value me, I cannot trust God.

- If God compromises my safety, I cannot trust God.

- If God is not good, I cannot trust God.

It could be easy to have a rapid response to these, but take caution and pause before jumping to answer Gen Z. Don't risk missing the mark in reaching Gen Z by offering something that lacks understanding of the audience. Consider visiting different chapters that discuss each of these ideas to prepare for answering the question *Can I trust God?*

- God accepts me as I am through the saving grace of Jesus Christ, and he also molds me into something new.

- God loves and values me, because he decided I was enough to make a way for atonement and redemption.

- God fully sees and knows me, and he will never leave those who put their faith in him. He is with me through all circumstances and situations.

- God is the definition of what is good and the source of all goodness, and following him means adjusting my lens of what is good to his lens.

Many Gen Zers have already answered the question this way: *No, I cannot trust God, or at least not the Christian God.* Remember, trust is built over time and with experiences. Gen Z lacks the time and practice to see God as trustworthy, or their lens has distorted the data. If we have earned the trust of our Gen Z friends, we can offer our lens. Here are some reasons I share with my Gen Z friends that I know I can trust God:

I can trust God because of the incarnation of Jesus Christ. God the Son has experienced human life. Though Jesus may not have experienced some of the exact circumstances you or I may face (Jesus never had a smartphone with social media), he did go through common human experiences. Jesus experienced loss, celebration, sorrow, friendship, loneliness, disappointment, joy, injustice, and more. God is not a stranger to the things we face. He is up close and personal, not a distant divine entity. He knows our struggles. God's with-ness is one reason we can trust him. God is with us in every situation, and he will never leave those who follow him.

I can trust God because he is unchanging. God is unchanging and reveals himself to us through Scripture and the Holy Spirit. I don't have to guess what kind of mood God is in or if he will be different today than yesterday. His consistency is reliable. The triune God is unchanging and is fully all things God is at all times. The God in the pages of the Bible is the same God today. The God of the Old Testament is the God of the New Testament. I *do* have to look for how he is consistent through different interactions and circumstances.

When we read the Bible, we are watching God interact with people at a specific point of history in a specific geography with a specific cultural context. Just as we have to unpack ideas of what trustworthy means for Gen Z, we have to unpack those same terms for what they meant to the people within Scripture. Then we are better able to see how these different visible facets of God are expressed in cultural ways, and how he interacts with us within our own cultural moment. God doesn't change, but culture changes, and God's consistent character meets us in our cultural moment.

I can trust God because he keeps his promises. God does what he says he is going to do. The Bible is full of examples of this. Jesus promised he would die and be raised to life again, and that is what happened. The kicker here is that God's timeline is not necessarily our timeline. The way he fulfills promises may look different than we expect. This is where the work of trust is stretched and grown. The prophecies of Isaiah were given about seven hundred years before Jesus' atoning death and resurrection, and the prophecies of Zechariah about five hundred years before. There were a few hundred years between the promise made and fulfilled, but God kept his promise. God is still keeping promises.

Finally, I can trust God because he has proven to be trustworthy in my life. Evidence of his trustworthiness has been built over time and experience. How will Gen Z know God is trustworthy if they do not spend time with him? How will they know if they do not pay attention to what God is doing? Can we help Gen Z by inviting them into our time and experience and sharing our stories with them?

Inviting Gen Z to become Worshipers is inviting them to practice trusting God. The act of worship represents and practices total reliance and dependence on God as a reflection of that trust, a living act of faith.

MORE THAN SONGS

A Worshiper offers their whole, authentic self to God as a disciple. According to Eric L. Mathis,

> Worship requires us to give God all that we are, including our worries, troubles, anxious thoughts, and fears, and it reminds us that the life, death, and resurrection of Jesus Christ hold our stories with the promise that in the end God will make all things well.[9]

Worship is the outward practice of the inward posture of being a Follower of God. Disciples of Christ learn to totally rely on God as Worshipers.

Worship is both expressive and formative: it expresses the cries of our heart to the Lord, and it provides a space to be changed and moved toward the Lord. It is not only reflective of bringing the inside worship outward into expression, but moves the outside act of worship inward, forming the posture of our hearts to adoration of and dependence on God. By practicing the feature of Worshiper as disciples of Christ, our identity as those who trust and follow Christ becomes increasingly pronounced.

Worshiping is more than singing songs, though a worship leader invites us to offer ourselves to God mostly in songs and hymns to remind us we are disciples who are Followers. That is a practice reflecting the inward position of trusting God. Worship goes beyond music, to the daily practice of offering ourselves to God, exhibiting our trust in him.

JESUS' AUTHENTIC WORSHIP

For a generation who is familiar with dual or hybrid identities, it is increasingly important to look at Jesus Christ as someone who is fully authentic and has complete integrity. Trust is built on being familiar with this authenticity. Jesus Christ is fully divine and fully human at the same time, and at all times, he provides an authenticity unlike anything else. Jesus' divine nature and human nature are not blended to create a new nature, but are two fully existing natures within one person. Jesus is authentically human and authentically God all of the time, and he also models what it looks like to be a Worshiper. When we look at Jesus demonstrating how to worship, we aren't looking for Jesus singing songs at church. We observe Jesus "as a perfect worshiper insofar as he offers his whole self to God in trust and hope."[10]

This trust is exhibited with Jesus in the wilderness (Matthew 4:1-11). The Spirit leads Jesus into the wilderness to be tempted by the devil. This breaks immediately with the idea that a trustworthy God would not lead you into difficulty or challenge (*Am I safe?*). What if we stopped after Matthew 4:1 and asked our Gen Z friends, "If God is good, why do you think the Spirit led Jesus to the desert to be tempted?" The desert does not feel like a safe place, but continue to join our Gen Z friends in wrestling with Scripture. "If God is good, what might be good or safe about the desert?" The Bible does not say the Spirit left Jesus; there must be something good or safe about being in the desert with God the Spirit. Wrestle here first with our Gen Z friends because it is difficult to move to trust in worship without dealing with such questions.

Gen Z may think doubt and trust cannot coexist. Remind them that doubt is not an enemy to trust, but that doubt tests trust. In doubt, we have an opportunity to put our reliance on God, or we can practice reliance on ourselves or others apart from God. In his commentary on Matthew, Dale Bruner says, "Doubt is the lever of temptation."[11] In his testing of Jesus, the devil attempts to create doubt in who Jesus is and whether he will trust and rely on God the Father. As we look at this passage with our Gen Z friends, ask them what kinds of doubts test whether they will trust or rely on God.

The devil challenges Jesus to bow down and worship him, to trust and rely on Satan instead of God the Father. Jesus responds, "Away from me, Satan! For it is written: 'Worship the Lord your God, and serve him only'" (Matthew 4:10). Jesus' words and actions reflect being a Worshiper of God, relying on and trusting God alone. He does not trade the goodness of God for the tangible, immediate, and temporary promises of the devil. The devil attempted to create doubt that would deteriorate trust in God, but even in his weakened state, Jesus' actions say, *I trust God the Father.*

We can point out to Gen Z where God keeps his promises in this passage. God keeps his promise to provide a way out of temptation: "God is faithful: he will not let you be tempted beyond what you can bear. But when you are tempted, he will also provide a way out so that you can endure it" (1 Corinthians 10:13). The Spirit is with Jesus. God keeps his promise to always be with us (Matthew 28:20; Psalm 16:9-11).

Being a Worshiper of God doesn't mean we don't have our own ideas and desires, but that we ultimately rely on and worship God with those ideas and desires. Being a Worshiper is about trading our own ideas and desires for the will of God. The Worshiper acknowledges who God is and lays everything at his feet, trusting God's goodness.

A TALK WITH GEN Z

In evangelism to Gen Z, we have to prove God's trustworthiness, and in discipleship, we have to teach them how to trust God. Gen Z is working with criteria for judging God's trustworthiness that we must become familiar with. When we hear a Gen Zer asking, *Can I trust God?* we might have to extend the question and ask, "Trust God to do what?" We may find out where our young friends are holding on to ideas of what they think God should do according to their values, longings, or wants.

We can even give permission to Gen Z to allow their doubts to test their faith. If my criteria for trust is that God will consistently answer my requests, prayers, and desires affirmatively with a yes, well then, God will most definitely not meet that criteria. If my criteria for trust is that God will never lead me to do something that is risky, uncomfortable, difficult, or even leads to suffering, well then, the Bible is full of stories demonstrating the very opposite, and thus, God does not meet that criteria either. It is important to clarify what we are saying when we say we can trust God.

Talk about trust in concrete terms. One way we can do this is by posing the sentence, "We can trust God to . . . ," and then fill in the blank. Unpack Gen Z's definitions of what trust means and how that trust is built or broken. Ask them to share stories about how God has met those standards or fallen short. Listen and understand (which also builds trust).

Putting your trust in God is an abstract concept that is probably helpful to explain in concrete terms and pair with a tactile experience, like writing a letter to God, or writing what we want to trust God with on a piece of paper and then burning it to show it is not in our control anymore. Slow down and engage an experience, rather than quickly offering a Bible verse about trust.

When we become a Follower of God, we become a Worshiper of God. Learning to worship God is learning to trust God. The invitation to follow God, to put your faith in God, or to trust God with your life now and forever is a big leap for Gen Z. They have been taught by their cultural upbringing not to trust. Lean in, respect the process, and keep sharing about and showing ways that God the Father, God the Son, and God the Holy Spirit are trustworthy.

Any proximity we can offer our Gen Z friends can help them see our reliance and dependence on God as a Worshiper. Let's share stories from our lives and explain what it means for us to trust God. Ask a Gen Z friend to notice God along with you. Say, "Remind me and help me notice what God is doing." Write the ways God has shown he is trustworthy on a note card, or a Post-it, or in a journal. Let's create a record of God's faithfulness with our Gen Zers. This takes time.

Gen Z is helping us get it right. Relationships deserve time, and Gen Z is worth it! This isn't just meeting together to do a Bible study, but sharing meals at the dinner table, going on walks, watching your kids' soccer games, and going to the grocery store. I have found Gen Zers from adolescence to adulthood enjoy doing these activities with an adult older than them who cares about them. They love being invited to share life together! More mentors of older generations are needed to disciple a fewer number of Gen Zers at a time. Gen Z will learn how to be Worshipers from other Worshipers, who will walk the journey together with them.

KEY IDEAS

Ask Gen Z: How do you know if you can trust someone?

Gen Z Question: Can I trust God?

Response: We can trust that God is who he says he is all the time; God is unchanging. The incarnation of Jesus Christ demonstrates God is *with* us. Jesus, in his full humanity, knows our struggles. We can trust God to keep his promises.

Result: Worshipers place total trust in and reliance on God. Worship is an outward expression of the inward trust in God the Father, God the Son, and God the Holy Spirit.

7

WHAT IS TRUE?

In 2015, "the dress" circulated the internet and social media, igniting arguments between friends and families. To some, the dress looked blue and black. To others, it looked white and gold. Last summer, I used a picture of "the dress" with a large group of young people in a discussion around the idea of truth. When the picture appeared on the screen, there was a collective groan, and immediately debates raged throughout the audience. A science experiment and social experiment was taking place before my eyes. Everyone got so stirred up that it took a few minutes for me to calm the room down. Why would one picture of a dress cause such conflict? People were arguing over what was true.

Truth has had an interesting journey. It once referred to something that was a fact, something you could count on—an unchanging compass to guide decisions, beliefs, or behaviors. For Gen Z, truth is a very different concept, and the cultural shift in the meaning of truth has created a different relationship between Gen Z and truth that previous generations may not fully understand.

A WALK WITH GEN Z

Gen Z's relationship with trust (*Can I trust you?*) is inter-twined with their relationship with truth (*What is true?*). Recall Gen Z's relationship with trust, and their distrust in media, power, authority, and institutions. If the media says something is true, there is almost always contradictory information on social media or the internet. Some information once considered true was later debunked—like, smoking is good for people with asthma. In my time as a mother, the argument of whether swaddling is good for a newborn baby has gone back and forth. The day after the 2024 presidential debate, fact-checking articles were posted from media outlets like NBC, CNN, PBS, ABC, CBS, the BBC, and so on, and high-lighted false "facts" shared by the candidates. There are also conversations around "deep fakes" and artificial intelligence. Digitally savvy Gen Z understands that what is presented as truth isn't always true.

Who can Gen Z trust? Who is telling the truth? And more importantly, is there a truth to be told?

Gen Z is justifiably careful. They are watching and discerning at all times as they develop their standards of what is good and bad. We should extend compassion and empathy for our next generation as they wrestle with their relationship with truth. Gen Z entered the world and was put in an impossible situation: do what is right, stand against what is wrong, and do so with no truth as a guide. They have their own personalized truths, but can never come against anyone else's personal truth. That's a tough spot.

Without understanding the complex and nuanced rela-tionship Gen Z has with truth, maybe we've jumped to, "The

Bible is true!" By saying this, we could think we provided a satisfactory answer, but we may have communicated something different than we intended. We may not be sharing good news, but contributing to an already distanced, possibly hostile, relationship with the Chrisitan faith. Why? What happened?

Truth as a weapon. Truth used to be seen as a source of peace. It was an anchor in which other ideas, values, and beliefs could be built around. Truth was a place where we could rest and take comfort. Truth was good news.

It's not the same for Gen Z. They have witnessed "truth" used as a weapon, used to exclude, harm, oppress, and excuse terrible behavior and actions. As truth was weaponized, truth became exclusive, seen by Gen Z as a tool to exclude. If you agree with or believe what is presented as truth, you are on the inside. If you disagree with or don't believe in what is presented as truth, you are on the outside. Being on the outside means your ideas and beliefs are rejected, shut out, and shut down. It could even lead to harm, oppression, or violence. This goes against Gen Z's value of acceptance.

A few years ago, I was on my way to speak to a couple hundred high school students and was walking through campus with my Bible in my hand. I was stopped by a student crossing my path (who was not attending the club meeting I was headed to). He pointed at my Bible, and said, "How dare you bring that harm on this campus." This student saw me as someone who was going to hurt others by opening my Bible on that campus. He saw the Bible as a weapon. We can follow this line of thinking to understand why truth is problematic for many in Gen Z: *You say the Bible is true + The Bible has been used to harm and oppress people = Truth can be harmful and oppressive.*

Today, that high school student is a young professional, carrying that belief with him as an adult.

In Gen Z's generational context, they may conclude, *If I don't want to participate in inflicting harm or oppressing others, I must reject the idea of truth.* This is an oversimplified and generalized formula to apply to a generation, but it points to the tension they feel under the surface. This is a generation who fights for social justice, cares about the environment, and is deeply principled in their values. All of which are part of the complexity around this conversation.

My truth sets me free. Gen Z grew up in a world where truth has been stripped of power and stability. For Gen Z, truth is individualized, and morality is fluid. Each person has the authority to decide what is true, right, and fair in any given situation. There has been a rise in a different iteration of new age spirituality that makes the individual the center of what is true.[1] Anyone can be their own god or have a customized "God." Gen Z can borrow from various belief systems to assemble a personalized spirituality and truth.

Truth can be talked about in personalized terms: *your truth, her truth, my truth,* and so on. *Psychology Today* posted an article titled "How to Find Your Truth," and advises the "letting go of relationships" with those who don't support "your truth."[2] This is how Gen Z has grown up both hearing about truth and talking about truth. When a Gen Zer hears the statement, "The Bible is true," they may respond, "That might be your truth, but not mine." Truth has been redefined to be a personal belief.

This complicates cross-generational conversations around truth. For previous generations, truth is understood to outrank personal belief. Truth should adjust our personal beliefs.

Universal truth is true everywhere, for everyone, at all times. Universal truth provides us with perspective outside of our own personal experience. Just because something is not personally experienced doesn't mean it's not true. Truth is objective.

Eric Mathis notes today's culture promotes expression from inside out, rather than being changed from the outside in:

> Our culture prizes individuals and encourages individuals to express themselves from the inside out; rarely does our culture place value on individuals who work to fit into communities of faith where they are formed from the outside in.[3]

Truth can change us from the outside in, but it does not have a chance to do so when we only focus inward. When truth is internally driven, we do not understand how external truth can change our feelings or how we experience the world around us.

How does Gen Z decide what is true? Actually, the more fitting question is, how does Gen Z decide what is true for them? If "the truth will set you free" (John 8:32), then to Gen Z, personalized truth leads to personal freedom. This is a generation that grew up singing with Elsa in *Frozen*, "No right, no wrong, no rules for me, I'm free!"[4] Freedom may be one of the most tightly held values for Gen Z. Anything that encroaches on personal freedom could be designated as not true.

For Gen Z, truth is pliable and situational. Is cheating on a test okay? Our Gen Zers may say, well no, unless the test was unfair or too difficult to pass on my own.[5] Is lying okay? A common Gen Z response is that this depends on the circumstances. If you're not going to get the job you want unless you lie on your resume, then it could be okay to lie.[6]

Maybe you are shaking your head in disbelief, but we have to remember, Gen Z grew up in a different time. They have seen headlines of science changed, and facts disproved. They've seen people canceled (and may have participated in the canceling) for stating something was true when that truth broke with cultural values. They have seen textbooks revised and books get banned. They watched the debates on how Covid-19 was handled, both on screen and in their local environments. Who was telling the truth? Often, Gen Z was left to fend for themselves, especially in digital spaces, to decide what was true during formative childhood and adolescent years, and into adulthood.

Feeling is believing. I was with two college students and abruptly asked them, "How do you decide what is true?" I had dived straight in with no lead-in, and was understandably met with stunned looks and wide eyes staring back at me. Thankfully, these Gen Zers knew me well enough to know I wasn't testing them; I was authentically curious. They both paused to think about the question, and I appreciated their intentional deliberation. It was a big question. The first Gen Zer to speak up noted, "If it is an expert that I trust, I probably believe what they say is true" (*Can I trust you?*). The second Gen Zer nodded and said, "If I have experienced it for myself, I know it's true."

Personal experience is hugely important to Gen Z. The arguments around the color of "the dress" were based on conflicting personal experiences: "I see blue and black" versus "I see gold and white." The sentiment is, *if I experience it, then it is true.* This is not unlike Thomas saying he needed to see the nail marks in Jesus' hands for himself before believing the truth that Jesus was alive. Thomas wondered what was true.

Maybe Thomas didn't believe the other disciples because he was too afraid to hope. Maybe his heart couldn't risk being disappointed again. Thomas had to feel Jesus' hands to believe Jesus was alive, and God entered Thomas's experience (*Can I trust you? Will you accept me? Is God good?*). We can introduce Thomas to our Gen Z friends as a disciple they can relate to.

I feel, therefore I am. Because experiences include feelings and emotions, these inform truth for Gen Z. Experiences, emotions, and "how I feel" have become a guiding authority.[7] They are connected to identity formation. Identity is something we feel: *This is who I feel I am, so it must be true.*[8] Identity is based on how each person sees themselves.[9] This layer is part of any conversation around sexuality or sexual identity and one reason why these conversations are so complex. Andrew Root uncovers how disagreement around what a person feels about his or her identity is seen as a violation: "If you refuse— or even overlook or dismiss—my expressions of my identity, you are assumed to have violently stripped me of meaning."[10]

Consider Jesus saying, "I am *the* way and *the* truth and *the* life" (John 14:6, emphasis added). The definite article, *the*, qualifies Jesus as the only way, the only truth, and the only life, not one among many options. What is the internal response from a Gen Zer? Does it cause tension? Discomfort? What do they have to wrestle with to engage with Jesus' statement? It is kind to our Gen Z audience to consider this. Throw in the rest of the verse to cause a real stir: "No one comes to the Father except through me." Gen Z could wonder: *Is God exclusive?*

We cannot assume we are delivering good news when we stand up and read that verse with authority to our next generation, assuming we have provided peace to our Gen Z audience.

Instead, we may have provided tension. It is not bad to offer places of tension, but we should be aware when we are doing it. It is a problematic thing to think we are offering peace, but offering otherwise. We must understand we are not closing the conversation but opening a new one that we are willing to lean into with our Gen Z friends.

Be patient, and don't expect our Gen Z friends to quickly jump to a different understanding of truth. First, we invite Gen Zers to consider the possibility that truth exists outside of us and our personal experiences. Then, we invite our Gen Z friends to consider the possibility that the Bible is full of truth. Could our Gen Z friends be open-minded enough to consider the possibility that God's truth is true?

Someone always gets hurt. Freedom sounds nice, and truth built around my sense of what makes me feel free sounds appealing. Extending the same freedom to yourself and to others sounds like a recipe for offering acceptance. You don't have to believe what I believe, and I don't have to believe what you believe. "You do you," as they say, and I can have a peaceful existence of guiding my own life.

This is a summary of the philosophy around truth that has engulfed Gen Z. It sounds good, but it quickly falls apart. What happens when these different ideas of what is true, right, or fair clash? If there is no universal truth or widely accepted moral standard, how do you decide which ideas and beliefs should rise to the top? Is there a truth that provides a direction for justice and truly loving our neighbor?

This worldview proves to be challenging when partnered with Gen Z's value for social justice. Justice requires an agreed-on truth expressed as a moral, value, or belief. For justice to exist, someone's version of truth has to be rejected. Someone has to be wrong. It must be extremely difficult to navigate the world this way, fighting for justice but also accepting everyone always. Gen Z has the challenge to fight for what is right and against what is wrong (which means rejecting something or someone), but without having a guiding universal truth. My goodness, I have anxiety imagining that kind of pressure, how could Gen Z not have anxiety? Without universal truth, Gen Z was left to fend for themselves. This is not good news and is not a pathway to a peaceful existence.

It is impossible to simultaneously value and accept all beliefs, values, and personalized truths. Some are just plain wrong and downright evil. Eventually, the qualifier was added, "as long as it doesn't hurt anybody." You do you, and if no one gets hurt, then you're alright. Is this possible? Is it possible to live holding up personal freedom and truth and not hurt anybody? I'm not convinced.

Anything outside of God's truth always hurts someone. That is the nature of sin: it destroys. I have witnessed friendships, marriages, and families divided and ended, leaving a trail of destruction and pain because someone was living "their truth." If we live our lives valuing ourselves, our truth and our freedom, over anyone else, the only outcome is hurt. This is not a recipe for acceptance or loving our neighbors. This is survival of the fittest. Making our own way and defining our own truth ultimately leads to a dead end, not to freedom.

This is one of the entry points for a conversation with Gen Z that reframes and redefines truth as a safe harbor, not a weapon. Truth is a resting place, where we can trade pressure for freedom. We practice patience here.

THE SHORT ANSWER: WHAT IS TRUE?

One of the great lies sold to Gen Z is that they can be the lord of their own lives and decide what is true for themselves. They see freedom as getting to do whatever you want, whenever you want, however you want, with whoever you want. If following God means losing my life (Matthew 16:25) or denying myself (Luke 9:23), it seems like a loss of freedom. Becoming a Follower of Jesus Christ means giving up being lord of one's own life. Understanding the cultural context of Gen Z, we can understand why this may be hard to accept. But this is not the whole truth.

We all are under the lordship of something: the lordship of sin or the lordship of Christ. Sin lies and convinces many that they are in control and free. Sin is sneaky like that. Make no mistake, serving ourselves is serving sin. Finding "my truth" to feed "my freedom" is living under the lordship of sin. Eugene Peterson, in *The Message*, paraphrases the "fruits of the flesh" (a.k.a. the fruits of sin's lordship in our lives) in Galatians 5:19-21:

> It is obvious what kind of life develops out of trying to get your own way all the time: repetitive, loveless, cheap sex; a stinking accumulation of mental and emotional garbage; frenzied and joyless grabs for happiness; trinket gods; magic-show religion; paranoid loneliness; cutthroat competition; all-consuming-yet-never-satisfied wants; a brutal temper; an impotence to love or be loved; divided homes and divided lives; small-minded and lopsided pursuits; the vicious habit of depersonalizing everyone into a rival; uncontrolled and uncontrollable addictions; ugly parodies of community. I could go on.

I read this to a small group of high school girls in a morning Bible study and asked them, "What part of this passage describes life right now or at your school?" They said, "All of it." Again, I shared this with a large group of high school students and asked the same question, "What part of this sounds like life right now?" They too said, "All of it." I explained that this is what the Bible says happens when we are finding our own way, looking for our version of what we think freedom is. I followed up with another question, knowing none of them had a relationship with Jesus: "Do you think you are free?" Their silence was stunning. They sat almost in shock at the realization *I'm not really free.*

Let's open the story of the prodigal son (Luke 15:11-24) with our Gen Zers, explaining that the son is to represent us and the father is to represent God. Highlight the lost son's search for what he thinks is freedom: life apart from his father. Many Gen Zers have concluded life apart from God is freedom. I like how the Jesus Storybook Bible says it: "He can go wherever he wants, do whatever he wants, be whoever he wants. He is the boss, he is free!"[11] As we follow the story, pause in the end and ask our Gen Z audience, "Do you think the son is free?"

When we help our Gen Z audience come to their own conclusion that they are not free, we can introduce real freedom. When we become a Follower of God, we are not giving up freedom, because we weren't really free. We are trading slavery to sin (Romans 6:16) for freedom. Jesus came to give life and life to the full, and his lordship in our lives provides full life. We are gaining freedom through God's grace and truth.

That is a long journey with Gen Z to get to a short answer. *What is true?* Our vehicle for knowing what is true is God's Word, the Bible, inspired by and divinely delivered through the Holy

Spirit. Yes, the triune God reveals himself in other ways, like general revelation and the works of the Spirit. God also chose to reveal himself to us through the written words of the Bible. God communicates the truths of who he is, who we are, of this world, and of the kingdom of heaven through Scripture. The Bible is *how* we know who Jesus is and what he did. It is God's intentional and infallible delivery of his message. It is where we learn about God, see Jesus, and get to know the Holy Spirit.

We also need to learn *how* to read the Bible. The Bible is rich with cultural context. This is why we are responsible to not only open the Bible with Gen Z, but to teach them how to engage with responsible hermeneutics and sound exegesis. It is not just sharing truths from the Bible in nice, compact thesis statements, but journeying together to get to that truth.

It is time to change the story that Gen Z is "biblically illiterate." I have witnessed older generations of Christians say, "The next generation doesn't know the Bible," and they throw up their hands and walk away from young people. This does not fix anything. It shuts Gen Z out. Let's teach them. Better yet, let's learn alongside them.

It is time not only to give Gen Z a compass of truth that leads to true freedom, but also show them how to use the compass so they can experience true freedom. Lean in, guide, steward, and walk with Gen Z. Don't just proclaim truth and expect it to be digested. Get into the thick of the questions, oppositions, and tension in the discomfort of the faith journey.

SAY WHAT YOU SAW

A Witness offers testimony by telling others what he or she has experienced. As a disciple of Christ and one who experiences freedom, we can share our story of freedom in God's truth. We testify to the truth of the Bible in practical, real-life, and personal ways. A Witness tells others about the good news of Jesus Christ and testifies to the work of the triune God from a personal perspective. Witnesses simply say what they saw, heard, felt, tasted, experienced, and so on. It is simply sharing their story.

JESUS AS WITNESS

Jesus was often a Witness to himself, sharing about the Messiah and Savior to the world while being the Messiah and Savior to the world. Jesus contextualized his testimony, engaging with his audience's questions and perspective, revealing different aspects of himself and his saving work:

- Jesus reads Scripture in the synagogue to a religious audience and announces that the prophecy he read is fulfilled through him (Luke 4:16-20).

- In Jesus' conversation with the Samaritan woman, she says she knows the Messiah (called Christ) is coming and will explain everything. Jesus responds, "I am he" (John 4:26).

- Jesus tells a crowd at Capernaum, "I am the bread of life. Whoever comes to me will never go hungry, and whoever believes will never be thirsty" (John 6:35).

Each of these statements were shared with different people in different settings facing different circumstances, and there are many more like this. We can see all the different ways Jesus testified about himself in the Bible, and we get a fuller picture of God the Son, as well as God the Father and God the Spirit.

Jesus forms a Witness. Jesus saw a man born blind (John 9:1-33), and his disciples asked if the man's blindness was either a result of his own sin or his parents' sin (John 9:1-2). This reveals the mindset of the time. Today, that mindset might be expressed as, "That's Karma, baby! What goes around comes around!" There are other Gen Z questions wrapped up in this passage:

- *Is God good?* (Would a good God cause an innocent man to be blind, or is this a version of God's justice?)
- *Do all people matter to God?* (Does God see and care about the blindness of this man?)
- *Will God accept me?* (Will God accept a man with sin?)

We can share this passage with our Gen Z friends and tackle any of these questions. There is also a larger wrestling with the truth behind these questions. The disciples are asking a question based on their limited experience and understanding of how things work in the world (just like the rest of us). We can invite our Gen Z audience to engage by asking, "Can you relate?" This is like "the dress." We don't have the full picture, and we may be deciding what is true based on incomplete information. For the disciples, it seemed obvious that something like blindness must be a result of sin.

Imagine being that blind man, viewed by others his entire life as someone who had done something terrible to be blind. Maybe he asked himself what he had done to earn the loss of his sight. Did God accept him? What was the truth?

Jesus says the blindness was not the result of the man's sin nor his parents' sin, but that the blindness was a way in which God's work could be displayed (John 9:3). Jesus revealed the truth, correcting the ideas of the people and disciples. Then, Jesus restored the man's sight by making mud with his spit and putting it on the man's eyes, and then sends the man away to wash the mud off in the Pool of Siloam (John 9:6-7). The man did so, and he could see!

Then, the formerly blind man becomes a Witness. He talks about what he experienced. One of the reasons I am drawn to the formerly blind man's witness is that it is clear he doesn't have all the answers, but he still shares his story:

- When others recognized him as the blind beggar they knew and argued about whether it was really him, he insisted, "I am the man" (John 9:9).

- He shared the series of events that led to his sight, and also shared that he did not know where Jesus was (John 9:10-12).

- When the man was brought before the Pharisees, he told them, "He put mud on my eyes, and I washed, and now I see" (John 9:13-15).

- Flabbergasted, because the healing took place on the Sabbath, the Pharisees ask the formerly blind man what he has to say about Jesus, to which he replies, "He is a prophet" (John 9:17).

- After more confirmation of the formerly blind man's identity, and more questions and demands from the Pharisees, the formerly blind man says, "Whether he is a sinner or not, I don't know. One thing I do know, I was blind but now I see!" (John 9:18-25).

The formerly blind man does not have all the answers. He simply shares his story, and that is what makes him a Witness.

He tells others what he knows is true from his experience ("I was blind, but now I see!"). He also acknowledges what he doesn't know. Use this to encourage Gen Z, who may worry, *Am I enough to be a Witness?* Tell your Gen Z friends that their story is enough for God to use.

But wait, there's more. In light of our conversations around cancel culture, I think Gen Z can empathize with the formerly blind man's experience with the Pharisees. The Pharisees insult the man and degrade him, attempting to devalue and discredit his testimony as a Witness. The formerly blind man answers them by being a Witness, sharing his story. The man argues that God listened to Jesus, so Jesus must not be a sinner, and that God must be with him. His proof is that his story is unique; no one had heard of a blind man gaining sight.

In the end, the Pharisees throw him out. They cannot listen anymore. They cannot reconcile the conflicting "truths" they are dealing with: the truth that a miracle has taken place on the Sabbath, and the truth that no work is to occur on the Sabbath. The Pharisees could not figure out how to rank these events in importance and validity. When we, and our Gen Z friends, experience rejection as Witnesses, we find friendship with the formerly blind man. The rejection he experienced continues today.

Did the formerly blind man fail as a Witness? It is not the job of the Witness to convince others to believe. That was not the formerly blind man's job. He served as a Witness to the work of Jesus Christ. He talked about what he knew from his experience, he spoke what he saw, and he readily acknowledged what he did not know.

Plot twist: because he faithfully told his story, the Pharisees were not the only ones who have heard the testimony of his

Witness or who have seen the change in his life. Imagine all the questions people asked. Imagine the days and weeks that followed as people observed this formerly blind man and talked with him. The Bible does not address all the people who heard the testimony of his Witness, but I have to imagine that many asked about Jesus, and maybe some began to believe in Jesus as a result of the Witness's testimony. This man's story is still being shared! We are reading his witness and are being changed by his testimony today! He may have been canceled by some, and so may we, but others may know truth and freedom in Christ because we were Witnesses.

The formerly blind man's testimony as a Witness was not a full presentation of the gospel. He didn't even have a full answer to who Jesus was, calling Jesus a prophet (John 9:17). He didn't make apologetic arguments or quote Scripture. The formerly blind man simply talked about his encounter with Jesus. That is what a Witness does. It is simple. It is authentic. It offers freedom.

Learning to be a Witness as a Follower of God is learning to share authentically—not having all the answers, but talking about what we have experienced with God.

A TALK WITH GEN Z

Gen Z is in a cultural moment designed for Witnesses. To put it in culturally translated terms, being a Witness as a disciple of Christ is sharing "my truth," which happens to be about *the* truth of Jesus Christ. Storytelling is becoming more and more integrated into the vernacular of the culture, and being a Witness also is "telling my story." It is not an apologetic for why the gospel is true or why the Bible is God's truth, or even why God is real. Proving why God is real or the Bible is true do not seem to be the most effective place to start a gospel conversation. Preparing for a debate leads to an argument, and preparing a lecture leads to not listening.

But it is difficult to argue with someone's story. In fact, arguing with someone's story is not culturally acceptable. An entry point to sharing the good news is sharing our story or sharing our truth, sharing our Witness testimony. It is an invitation for others to come and see for themselves.

My friend Jim's father was in the FBI. Due to his expertise, Jim's father often appeared in court as an expert witness. His testimony was presented and understood as truth. There were also other witnesses, everyday people, who testified in court. Their job was simply to tell their story, talk about their experience, and share what they saw. Their words were not meant to be presented as absolute truth, but a step toward the truth. Being a Witness as a disciple of Christ means being both a witness and an expert witness. We share our story as everyday people. As we spend more time following God, our "expertise" in God increases, and we can be viewed as expert witnesses.

Part of growing as a Witness is learning to share our story not only in words, but also with our lives. This is an invitation for Gen Z to live into their value of authenticity: living as a Witness who is a Follower of God is living authentically!

One of the reasons Gen Z has seen a weaponizing of truth is that truth (or biblical theology) was expressed in bad, harmful actions and practice. Gen Z concluded, *Truth is harmful, and harmful practice is a result of bad theology.* A Witness has an opportunity to display good practice through biblical living, living out truth in a visible and tactile way. This way of life is living proof that the gospel is true and God's Word shared in Scripture is true.

Being a Witness complements Gen Z's generational culture, but that does not mean Gen Z disciples know how to share their testimonies. We can help our Gen Z friends to understand and verbalize their story, while also walking with them and becoming visible testimonies to the truth of the gospel of Jesus Christ. We can be like the formerly blind man, saying: "Look, I don't know a lot about God, I just know I was blind and now I see."

We begin by sharing our stories, and by finding other older Followers of Christ to share theirs. Let's ask our Gen Z friends which parts of the stories resonate with them, and which parts they have more questions about. Then, we can encourage Gen Zers to tell their stories.

I teach young people to narrow their story to three to four sentences. This doesn't capture everything (neither did the testimony of the formerly blind man), but it is a brief, honest, and clear mini-story that can open the door to further conversation. Gen Zers can be ready to be a Witness at any moment, giving an opportunity for others to hear more. We can teach Gen Z that their testimonies are not a weapon. Their testimonies bring hope and freedom.

Being a Witness can also be the way we approach sharing the gospel with Gen Z: "Whether or not you believe in God, or believe that the Bible is true, all I know is that my life completely changed when I gave my life to Christ. And I have story after story to tell." A single generation who shares their authentic Witness testimony can change the world.

KEY IDEAS

Ask Gen Z: How do you know something is true? Do you think you are free?

Gen Z Asks: What is true?

Response: God is the source of truth. He shares truth through the Bible. To reject God's truth for what we think is freedom is actually not freedom at all, but living under the lordship of sin. God's truth is the way to be free.

Result: Witnesses share personal testimony, in words and actions, to what they have experienced. It is sharing "my truth," which happens to be the truth of the gospel of Jesus Christ.

8

AM I SAFE?

"I think we were sold a wrong idea of safety."

I was blown away, sitting at my kitchen table across from a Gen Z young woman. I tried to remain cool, but I was taken off-guard by her counter-generational reflection that was vastly more mature than her age would indicate. I asked her to tell me what she meant. She said,

> I feel like we have been told safety is never being uncomfortable or being sad, or never taking risks, or even never failing, but I don't think that's realistic. I think it's all an illusion. We will never be truly safe in that way, and I'm not sure we are supposed to chase that idea. We are trying to grab something that doesn't exist.

This didn't come out of nowhere. New to faith, this young woman had been coming over to my house to study the Bible together with me for almost a year. She had noticed that the stories of Scripture did not match the ideas and values around safety she had grown up with. People in the Bible encountered all kinds of dangerous and risky situations.

I hear the word *safe* mentioned a lot, especially in places where young people are: "We want school to be safe," "We want this to be a safe space," or "Show up as a safe adult." At some point, safety became king. Safety became a pinnacle value of society. Safety grew into such a big conversation that there are different categories of safety for specific conversations: psychological safety, learner safety, inclusion safety, contributor safety, challenger safety, and so on. Safety became steeped in our environment.

Around 2015, I started evaluating the success of events for teenagers by asking three questions: (1) *Did kids have fun?* (2) *Did kids hear about Jesus?* and (3) *Did kids feel safe?* Prior to 2015, I had only focused on the first two. Safety had now entered my vocabulary. Where did it come from? Let's journey back in time to when Gen Z was much younger, being raised to value safety.

Some think this focus on safety resulted from the childhood experience of Generation X. When Gen X was growing up, it was the first time a missing child appeared on a milk carton or kidnappings were featured on the news. "Stranger Danger" entered the cultural vernacular as we began to understand that there were adults who wanted to harm children. Growing up, my own family had a secret password, so that if anyone I didn't know tried to pick me up, that person would have to say the secret password (this was never an actual scenario I found myself in). One message had become clear to Gen X: bad things can happen to kids. As Gen X and Millennials became parents to their own children, they focused on keeping kids safe in a dangerous world. It began with physical safety, but the definition of "safe" has expanded.

The heart of safety is a desire to see our kids not get hurt, whether it is physically hurt, emotionally hurt, or psychologically hurt.[1] I get it. When my kids cry, even if it is over nonsense (my youngest cried yesterday because he wanted to drink water, but he had rinsed with fluoride and had to wait for thirty minutes), it drains my physical and emotional battery. It wears on me, and I become frayed. When my kids are in pain, the pain does not stop there. I am in pain with them and for them. Maybe that's part of the heart of safety: *I don't want to hurt.* Consider how Gen Z was raised, and how adults may have protected them from experiencing pain. According to Lisa Damour, "Emotional pain promotes maturation."[2] How does protecting Gen Z from all pain shape where they are today?

The focus on safety surrounded Gen Z as small children and it continues to surround Gen Z into adulthood, deeply entrenching the value of and longing for safety.[3] This results in the question *Am I safe?* This question of safety (*Am I safe?*) is intertwined with Gen Z's other questions:

- If God is good, then I am safe.
- If I am enough for you, without risk of not being enough, then I am safe.
- If you accept me, then I am safe.
- If I can trust you, then I am safe.

The inverse is also true. For example, if you are a safe person, then I can trust you. If you are safe, you will accept me.

A twentysomething Gen Zer asked me, "Do older genera-tions know what it's like to feel safe?" I, a Gen Xer, took time to think, and I responded, "I don't know, at least in the way Gen Z understands 'safe.'" Perhaps older generations aren't looking to be safe in the same ways, so we have a more difficult time identifying when we are safe. Through the question proposed to me, I realized I needed to work to understand safety from a Gen Z lens.

A WALK WITH GEN Z

According to Jonathan Haidt in *The Anxious Generation*, Gen Z was raised in a time in which they were taught that the world is dangerous:

> This is the world in which Gen Z was raised. It was a world in which adults, schools, and other institutions worked together to teach children that the world is dangerous, and to prevent them from experiencing . . . risks, conflicts and thrills.[4]

Rather than teach Gen Z how to navigate those dangers, Haidt says adults, schools, and institutions like churches taught Gen Z how to avoid those dangers.[5] Gen Z wasn't just avoiding physical danger, but was encouraged to avoid experiencing negative feelings altogether.

Safety was built into the world of Gen Z. Safety became a human right, and any compromise of safety became a violation of that right, violating that person. People deserve to feel safe. In many ways, safety is defined as guaranteed happiness, comfort, and even success for each person. As mentioned earlier, Jean Twenge found that Gen Z is asking, "Is it safe?" and have a longing "to feel 'safe' all the time."[6] If we move this question to a personal reflection, it becomes *Am I safe?* When we discuss faith, it becomes *Is God safe?*

The actual generational definition of safety for Gen Z is a difficult thing to get one's arms around because it is both wide and narrow. It is wide because it includes physical safety, emotional safety, psychological safety, spiritual safety, intellectual safety, safety from embarrassment, safety from failure, safety from risk, safety from disagreement, safety from being uncomfortable, and so on. It includes being safe from challenging circumstances, obstacles, and difficult feelings. Being "safe" includes a wide range of topics, experiences, and parameters. The definition of what is "safe" is also narrow, because each person has a specific, individualized definition of what it means to feel safe.

A high school student shared with me that she doesn't like coming to our small group Bible study because she feels too exposed. The intimacy of a smaller group makes her feel unsafe, and she prefers the larger group activities, where she can blend in with the crowd and have an opportunity to observe before participating. Similarly, there are students who start with our small group Bible study first, even if they don't believe in the Bible, simply because it is smaller than our large group events. People learn their names. They are seen. The noise level is quieter. They feel safer starting small.

Survey some Gen Zers and ask them, "What kind of environment or person makes you feel safe?" Each will have personal requirements to feel safe, and likely a personal definition of safety. Some need a crowd to feel safe, and some need a small group to feel safe. Some need to be called on to feel safe to have the space to speak, and some feel safe never being acknowledged from up front. Some need assigned teams to feel safe, and some need to choose their teams. This is challenging, to say the least.

Illusion of safety. Here's the twist: complete safety is impossible to achieve at all times. Gen Z is searching for safety they will never find in this world. With the definitions of "safe" that Gen Z is operating under, so much depends on external people and factors.

There is almost no agency or control over one's own safety. Gen Z is familiar with the concept of "triggering" or "being triggered," terms referring to negative emotional responses or psychological reactions to external factors. Safety can include being safe from having my feelings hurt, or from being emotionally disrupted by something someone says to me personally or by something that is said from up front while I sit in the audience. But there is no control over what others say, or where anyone will be when those things are said. For Gen Z, it can make life feel like walking through a field of landmines, not knowing if the next step will be an explosion. Gen Z was given a value impossible to achieve: *be safe always.*

Am I a safe person? When working with the next generation, I also feel like I'm walking through landmines, not knowing if something I say or do will unintentionally and accidentally breach someone's sense of safety. Then, boom! The relationship is compromised! The conversation is over. To be able to both know each person's definition of safety and be able to simultaneously provide it is a daunting, impossible task for any pastor, practitioner, or parent.

Because of this personalized definition of what it means to be safe, and because safety is a high value for Gen Z, we have to be careful when and how we use the word *safe*. I would caution against saying, "This is a safe place for you," or "Don't worry, I am a safe person," without defining in concrete terms exactly what we mean. Why? If we promise safety with a particular definition in mind, but it is not the same definition as our audience, and we violate their definition, we've not only proved we are not safe, but we've also proved we are not trustworthy (*Can I trust you?*). *Safe* is a word that must be defined for the context of the conversation or the situation, or we risk unintended outcomes.

This value of safety has caused a dichotomy: safe is good, and unsafe is bad. Thus, safe people are good and unsafe people are bad. There isn't really an in-between. We can be either labeled safe or unsafe by our Gen Z friends. Because we do not know each person's definition of what it means to be safe, we can quickly be moved unknowingly into the "unsafe" category by our Gen Z friends. Maybe I am unsafe because I asked a question that made someone feel put on-the-spot. Maybe I'm unsafe because I asked someone not to use bad language. Maybe I am unsafe because I laughed at something I thought was a joke, but wasn't. Maybe I am unsafe because I am a Christian. Whether or not I am safe impacts the opportunity to share the gospel. It is why I wrestle so much with how to understand and engage the question, *Am I safe?*

This "safe is good" and "unsafe is bad" cultural system becomes even more difficult to navigate when we enter a conversation around faith.

'Course he isn't safe. Safety is one of the places Gen Z gets stuck when it comes to the Christian faith. To Gen Z, the Christian faith looks risky and dangerous. It requires putting your trust in God, who you cannot see, touch, or explain. Gen Z observes public hostility directed at Christians and judgment of men and women of faith, and Gen Z doesn't want to be the subject of that public hostility or judgment for following God. The Bible is filled with faithful men and women in wild and dangerous situations. I can't blame Gen Z for their hesitancy. We can't just say, "You're safe with God! It's safe to give your life to Christ!"—not with their current definition of safe.

Those familiar with the book *The Lion, the Witch, and the Wardrobe* may already be thinking of Mr. Beaver's words regarding Aslan. When Susan asks if Aslan, the God figure in the story, is safe, Mr. Beaver responds, "Who said anything about safe? 'Course he isn't safe. But he's good. He's the King, I tell you."[7]

He isn't safe? Yikes! This quote is not an answer to the question, but it could be the start of a dialogue. When we unpack it with our Gen Z friends, we can ask them, "What do you think about that?" We cannot just share Mr. Beaver's words, end the conversation, and walk away thinking we have shared good news in addressing the questions of Gen Z. Without explanation or conversation, we could push away Gen Z, present a reckless, uncaring God, and set off a collision of values.

For Gen Z, safety is good. If God is not safe, God is not good. If God is good, God is safe. But God's definition of *safe* does not always line up with Gen Z's cultural and individual ideas of safety. How do we resolve that God is good, but God is not necessarily our version of safe? We have to show and explain that God's definition of what is safe is what is *good*.

THE SHORT ANSWER: AM I SAFE?

Answering this question is similar to how we answer the question *Is God good?* We have to address the current definitions of safety, and then reframe safety through a biblical lens. Let's examine the Gospels with Gen Z to find places where people seemed to be in unsafe and risky situations, but were safe with Jesus.

Zacchaeus gets out of the tree (Luke 19:5-19). Zacchaeus found a safe place from which to see Jesus: up in a tree. The crowd likely despised Zacchaeus for his thieving, lying, tax-collecting ways. It was safer for him to hide in the tree. Shame and rejection waited for him outside of that tree with the crowd. However, Jesus invites Zacchaeus to come down and invites himself over for a meal. Zacchaeus has to climb down into the unsafe crowd. The safety Jesus offers is being fully seen, known, loved, and received by the triune God. We will not be rejected when we come to God to give him our lives. Safety is in the assurance of who we are in Christ: beloved, adopted, redeemed, ransomed, restored, and, ultimately, resurrected.

Peter walks on water (Matthew 14:22-33). The disciples are at sea in a boat, which is being tossed by high winds. Jesus invites Peter to get out of the boat and walk to him on the water while the wind and waves rage. That sounds risky and il-logical, and it sounds "unsafe." Inside the boat is safe; outside the boat is unsafe. Peter gets out though, and walks on the water toward Jesus, but begins to sink when he realizes the storm is continuing around them. Jesus immediately catches Peter. Peter was always safe with Jesus. Peter's ability to walk on water did not rely on how good, faithful, knowledgeable, or strong he was. He relied instead on God the Son. True safety is not safety from difficulty or hardship; true safety is that God is with us in the difficulty or hardship. Safety is in God's with-ness, his fellowship with us while we face risk, failure, discomfort, disagreement, embarrassment, or pain.

The disciples hide and Thomas doubts (John 20:19-29).
The disciples had watched the Messiah be arrested and die a criminal's death. They were likely next, so they hid. Jesus later appears to them, alive. He does not tell them to keep hiding, but gives them the Holy Spirit, and empowers them to do his work. Thomas was not there, though, and had not seen the risen Christ. He did not believe the other disciples' testimony, and it was safer for him to doubt. When Jesus appears next to Thomas, he invites Thomas to explore his hands and side without rebuke. Jesus' scars are not absent from his resurrected body, but are proof of what had taken place, and proof to Thomas that this is truly Jesus. True safety is assurance that death will not have the final word. True safety is knowing and trusting that God is not reckless or wasteful, but that he uses all things for good. True safety is not hiding but living with the Holy Spirit and doing the Lord's work. True safety is bringing our doubts and questions to a God who receives them.

When we talk about these Gospel accounts, we need to draw out the themes of safety. Last week, I heard from one youth worker who said three different high school students had approached him after a message to say, "That hit different." He used the Zaccheus encounter to talk about Jesus being safe and accepting. He had never used this kind of language before, but he did that night and realized, *This really matters.*

We could go on and on with examples not only from the Gospels, but throughout the Bible that reflect what true safety in God looks like in the face of what seem to be unsafe circumstances. Story after story, we see God's followers facing, by all earthly accounts, unsafe circumstances. Time after time, they are truly safe in God in unpredictable, unimaginable, and extravagant ways. Even the not-so-happy endings rest in God's safety, like Stephen, who in the moments leading to his death was filled with the Holy Spirit and saw God with Jesus next to him (Acts 7:55-60). Just because a man builds his house upon a rock doesn't mean the storm doesn't come (Matthew 7:24-25), but it does mean the house on the rock won't be crushed by the storm.

Let's help our Gen Z audience begin to grasp the spiritual realm as we delve into the question, *Am I safe?* As Followers of God and readers of the Bible, we understand we have an enemy in Satan. With an enemy prowling around like a lion, looking for someone, maybe me, to devour (1 Peter 5:8-9), am I safe? God not only provides armor to stand against our enemy (Ephesians 6:11), but is also stronger, more powerful, and ultimately victorious against our enemy (Colossians 2:15). Safety is assurance in God's victory. God's victory includes victory over death. Even if the body is killed, we are forever alive with God. Safety is assurance that this strong, powerful, victorious God loves *us*! As we become a Follower, safety is assurance that nothing will ever separate us from the love of God through Christ Jesus (Romans 8:38-39).

Intimacy with the triune God not only is the safest place to be, but it also reveals a new definition of what true safety is through God.

DON'T BE A GOLD DIGGER

As Followers of God, Gen Z grows in the understanding of God's safety and develops courage as Intercessors. An Intercessor enters prayer on behalf of others, intervening for the sake of their neighbor.

Fear can drive out safety, but in prayer, we can experience God's love driving out fear (1 John 4:18). The Intercessor becomes increasingly familiar with approaching God on the throne of grace and can be bold in doing so (Hebrews 4:16). Prayer is a place where God reminds us of his deep love for us, of our identity as his beloved ones, and of his love for others (*Am I enough?*).

The Intercessor seeks to know and follow the Lord's will. Prayer is led by the Holy Spirit, providing the Intercessor the words to pray (Romans 8:26-27). When prayer is led by the Holy Spirit, it is not limited by my human logic or constrictions, or by my ideas of what is safe. Prayer moves me past those things. Prayers become big, faith-stretching, hope-filled, and bold—prayers that move us past the idea of being "safe" in our worldly terms. At the same time, these are the safest prayers because they are led by God.

The goal of the Intercessor is simply to be obedient in the act of prayer, not to pray well enough for God to give what is prayed for. God is not a magic genie granting wishes. The pitfalls for Gen Z are in thinking that if they don't get what was desired, they were either (1) not faithful enough in prayer, or (2) not praying God's will. But there may be times the Holy Spirit leads us to pray simply to lead us in obedience to God in the form of intercessory prayer, regardless of the outcome.

When it comes to prayer, some of my high school students and I like to say, "Don't be a gold digger." It's our way of saying, "Don't pray just to get stuff." Don't obey God just to obtain the blessing. Intercede in prayer because it is part of obedience. Sure, that's not a very safe answer. It is actually pretty risky. It doesn't fit into the ideas of Santa Claus and karma, or even the prosperity gospel: *If I do good, good will come to me.* We can easily slide into the idea that if I pray hard and faithfully, a good God will grant my request. (This goes back to judging God's goodness by my standards, rather than discerning what is good through God.) An Intercessor learns to trust God's direction regardless of the outcome. Success or safety on our terms is not guaranteed. An Intercessor obeys by praying, trusting God's goodness regardless of the answer to that prayer. An Intercessor, as a Worshiper, puts full trust in and reliance on God. In practicing prayer, an Intercessor develops courage.

Sounds scary, right? An Intercessor is changed by God through prayer so that this obedience flows out of their life of faith. It is through prayer that our idea of what is safe becomes formed and molded by God. It becomes not so scary the more we practice intercessory prayer led by the Holy Spirit.

JESUS AS INTERCESSOR

Jesus is an Intercessor for us even now (Romans 8:34; Hebrews 7:25). He is described as our advocate with God (1 John 2:1). That is another way to think of the feature of Intercessor, as an advocate to God for those we pray for. We cannot see how Jesus currently intercedes for us, but Jesus models being an Intercessor in the Gospels by praying intercessory prayers.

Big, bold hope. Jesus prays for his disciples (John 17:6-19) and for all believers (John 17:20-26) before his arrest, trial, and death on the cross. Jesus prays for protection over the disciples, for unity with God the Father, that they would have joy, to sanctify them, and once again for protection, this time from the evil one. In his prayer for all believers, Jesus prays for unity with God, that all believers would become a Witness to others that Jesus is sent by God and is God, for glory to be given to believers, and that all believers will ultimately be with Jesus and see his glory. These are big prayers for others.

This is an indicator of what it means to be an Intercessor: praying bold and big prayers for others. These prayers are also consistent with the Word and work of God in the Gospels. These prayers speak hope of what could be or what will be. In Jesus' intercessory prayers, he recognizes reality ("I will remain in the world no longer, but they are still in the world" in John 17:11 and "I have given them your word and the world has hated them" in John 17:14) and moves toward God in it. Jesus' prayers are directional toward God the Father for the movement of the disciples and all believers toward God.

In the jungle. Jesus demonstrates that being an Intercessor is going to God on behalf of others, even when they are not asking to be prayed for. When Jesus is on the cross, he acts as Intercessor, praying, "Father, forgive them, for they do not know what they are doing" (Luke 23:34). The people Jesus is praying for do not understand their actions and are not asking for prayer. They do not see how they are treating the King of kings and Creator of all. Jesus' prayer is a prayer for mercy for those who are not asking for mercy.

Some see God as an unfair, unjust judge, punishing those who had no chance to hear the gospel. This is often expressed in a question: What about the people in the remote jungle who have never heard about Jesus? Will God punish them? Jesus' prayer displays God's heart for all people, even those who are guilty, but do not know what they are doing. Jesus' prayer also shows us how to respond as Intercessor. If our Gen Z friends are concerned for the people in remote places of the world who have never heard about Jesus facing God's ultimate judgment, will they be Intercessors on their behalf? We can follow the example of Jesus, to pray for those who do not know what they are doing. We can pray they would come to their senses like the lost son and look for home with a God they do not know (Luke 15:17-18). We can pray for forgiveness to find them.

A TALK WITH GEN Z

It might be easy for many of us to think, *I'm not good at praying*, whether we are Gen Z or any other generation. I have said it about myself many times (along with, "I don't like praying out loud"—and in my line of work, I have to pray out loud . . . a lot). Some of the features of a disciple come easily to us, and others don't. Some features of a disciple come easily to others, and others don't. Because of that, we can make the mistake of thinking that if praying does not come easily, then we must not be good at being an Intercessor, so we shouldn't pray.

As we teach our Gen Z friends how to pray, prepare for many questions: *How do I pray? Why do I pray? How do I focus? How do I know I'm praying God's will?* Press in to see if these questions are being presented as fears and obstacles, or if they are rooted in curiosity pointed toward growth. More and more, I understand prayer and intercession must be taught, modeled, and practiced, just like you would practice any other new skill. Listening to the Holy Spirit is a skill to be explained and attained. These things must be broken down into concrete, digestible, actionable steps or they remain a mysterious, ungraspable aspect of faith. Don't get me wrong, there is mystery involved, but God does not hide from us how to be an Intercessor, as we see in Jesus and other parts of the Bible.

After sitting with many of our Gen Z friends, I can testify that intercessory prayer, generally, is not being taught. It is not being passed down. I was leading a staff meeting and asked, "Who taught you about spiritual battle and how to engage with it?" Many named a specific person or mentor. They told stories of being with someone who explained and modeled spiritual battle. Actually, everyone listed a person, except for the one Gen Zer in the room. He answered last, mostly because his response did not match his older cohorts in the room. Who taught this young staff person about spiritual battle and how to engage with it? He answered, "TikTok."

He explained he didn't know where to go with his questions about spiritual battle, and the quickest and easiest way to find answers was to search TikTok. Whether that response makes us laugh or cringe, it communicates how important it is for older generations to be in mentoring relationships with younger ones. We have to be with our Gen Zers to show them. They learn by listening to and watching us pray next to them. It is also important to take these spiritual and abstract concepts, like being an Intercessor, and find a way to explain, translate, and demonstrate them for the sake of our next generation.

Getting the ball rolling. One way to help Gen Zers engage with the Holy Spirit is to provide space to listen to the Holy Spirit. Start small. Ask them to pause for thirty to sixty seconds, and write down names of people they want to pray for. After doing this with Gen Zers, we get to explain, "You have listened to the Holy Spirit! Those names didn't come out of nowhere and they aren't random. You know so many people, and yet those are the ones that came to mind, and they were clear enough for you to recognize and write down!"

Every time I do this with our Gen Zers, the next question quickly comes: How do I know what to pray for? Sometimes we know what is going on in the lives of those written down on our list, and sometimes we don't. Again, this is an opportunity to practice learning how to rely on the Holy Spirit to guide us in prayer. Let's invite our Gen Z friends to take a moment, a few seconds, a minute, or more, to be silent and listen.

Listening is a term that can be confusing for many Gen Zers, because we are not necessarily listening with our ears for audible direction in prayer (personally, I have never experienced this phenomenon). We must explain to our Gen Z friends what we mean by the word *listen* during this exercise of praying for the names on their lists: to quiet their brains, ask the Holy Spirit how to pray, and pay attention to a sentence or word that may pop up in their minds. Not everything that comes into our mind is from the Holy Spirit, and so we offer ourselves as a guide to help our Gen Z friends decipher and discern what they "hear." How do we know the sentence or word is from God or is God's will? I'm not sure we know all the time, but we can coach our Gen Z friends to identify if that sentence or thought is consistent with who God is in the Bible. That is a good indicator we are at least not praying contrary to God.

Prompts for prayer. Don't assume that becoming an adult equates to a level of prayer competency. From adolescence to adulthood, many Gen Zers do not know how to pray or be comfortable praying with others because they were not taught or given space to practice. We can pray out loud with our Gen Z friends so they can see and hear how we pray.

Another way to practice prayer with our Gen Z friends is to give them words. For example, I have begun times of prayer by providing our Gen Zers a list of prayer prompts. These are brief prayers typed out on a sheet of paper, and I say, "If you are unsure of how to pray, or maybe would like some ideas on how to pray for your friends, maybe pick one or two from here to pray." It's more like a safety net for young people who don't know how to be an Intercessor quite yet. We can create a list of prompts for whatever the focus is for our time of prayer. Here are some of the prompts I currently provide Gen Zers when we pray for friends:

- Help our paths cross. I pray I am quick to listen and reach out, but also that I am present, that I slow down, put my phone away, look my friend in the eyes, and show them I am here for them.

- Give me an encouraging word for my friend, so that maybe my friend will know God is there.

- Please prepare my friend's heart to hear about you, know you, and follow you.

- Help me see the obstacles, the things that stand in the way of my friend coming to places they will hear about Jesus. Help me see how to help remove those obstacles.

- I pray for transformation in my friend's life—that it would be full of hope, light, joy, peace, and [fill in the blank with another word if you like].

- Please use the trouble in my friend's life to direct them toward you, not for discouragement. I pray against discouragement and hopelessness because that is not what you designed life to be.

- Give me courage for the moment I need to invite my friend to talk about Jesus or invite my friend to church, even if it means inviting them a few times.

These are just a few ideas to get the ball rolling. Perhaps, the Holy Spirit will provide words that are not on this list of prompts at all!

We start small, we provide tools, and we model prayer out loud with our Gen Z friends. Maybe we learned to pray by listening to others pray. Maybe we learned from reading the prayers of others in the Bible. The point is, we cannot expect our Gen Zers to understand how to be an Intercessor on their own. Praying together, with Intercessors side by side, the older generations with the younger ones, we all move toward understanding what it means to be safe in God, and discard the false ideas of safety that encroach on big, faith-filled intercessory prayer.

KEY IDEAS

Ask Gen Z: What kind of environment or person makes you feel safe?

Gen Z Asks: Am I safe? (Am I safe with God?)

Response: God provides a different definition of what it means to be safe. It is not safety from hardship, risk, or even suffering. It is safety in fellowship with a God who will never leave or forsake those who follow him. God fully sees and knows us, and he accepts us when we give him our lives. Then, nothing can separate us from God and his love. God is not reckless with our lives but uses everything intentionally for his purposes.

Result: We practice being Intercessors, praying for others. As Intercessors, we begin to understand God's definition of what it means to be safe in him, guided by the Holy Spirit.

9

WHAT NOW?

Tomorrow we will likely interact with a Gen Zer. They could be behind the counter at a coffee shop, working out at the gym, in our churches, at our workplaces, walking through campus, or even in our homes. We may get a text or DM (direct message) within the next hour from a Gen Zer in our life. With all we know now, what do we do next?

When we began, I proposed that if we understood the questions Gen Z is asking and the context around those questions, we would be able to answer them in evangelism and discipleship. How do we do that?

Approach evangelism and discipleship by beginning to understand the questions Gen Z is asking, and by answering those questions with the good news of Jesus Christ. For example, instead of deciding what Gen Z needs to know about the incarnation of Jesus Christ, and then telling them about the incarnation, figure out how the incarnation answers their questions. Instead of deciding what Gen Z needs to know about sin and then telling them about sin, we figure out how to discuss sin in a way that answers their questions. We continue this pattern, this practice, with all parts of the gospel in discipleship conversations.

It starts with reading the Bible with eyes for Gen Z. Keep the seven questions we discussed in mind: *Is God good? Do all people matter to God? Am I enough? Will you accept me? Can I trust you? What is true?* and *Am I safe?* One way I have done this is by keeping a little worksheet next to me while I read the Bible (see table 1). It helps me process the passage with eyes for Gen Z.

Table 1. My worksheet for reading the Bible with a Gen Z lens

Gen Z Values	Which question does this passage address?	What is the response or the good news?
Is God good?		
Am I enough?		
Will you accept me?		
Do all people matter to God?		
Can I trust you?		
What is true?		
Am I safe?		

I refer to those questions quite a bit to remind myself to look for the ways the Bible engages those questions, or the context around those questions. It requires active discipline to help my brain read Scripture in a different way, with a different purpose and a different lens. I am working to read the Bible with a Gen Z lens.

This is not about changing, updating, or trading traditional, orthodox theology for a new version. It is not moving away from a high view of Scripture, and it's not creating a watered-down version of Christianity. It is simply a process of looking at the Bible to figure out how it answers today's questions. It is finding how our theology satisfies the questions of Gen Z. It is connecting today's generation with a robust understanding of God, the Bible, and the life of faith as a disciple of Jesus Christ.

This is also not spoon-feeding and babying Gen Z or giving permission to a generation to not know their Bibles or be immature in their faith. (These are the arguments I often hear from older generations of Christians who oppose changes in contextualization for Gen Z.) We don't shake our fists in the air and complain about Gen Z and treat the Christian faith like a sink-or-swim situation. The next generation is both under our care and is our neighbor. We are invited to know the joy of loving and believing in Gen Z the way God does.

This is about thinking crossculturally, like missionaries to a foreign land of youth, where we once belonged, but now are strangers. We have to recognize that we are not speaking the same language as our next generation. We don't change our theology or our Bibles to engage Gen Z, but we do change our methods. We figure out how to share these things in a language and with a method that makes sense to Gen Z.

The gospel and discipleship we experienced was contextualized for us; we just may not have realized it at the time. Now, we must have a deeper and wider understanding of the triune God, and of our Bibles, the gospel, and discipleship, in order to contextualize our message for Gen Z.

As I have gone back to read Scripture with a lens for Gen Z, two things have happened. First, I am seeing how a generation's questions are answered in Scripture. Second, my appreciation and amazement for God's Word has grown even deeper than before!

FAMILIAR PASSAGES WITH NEW EYES

Gen Z's questions are addressed in the Bible, often in passages that I have read countless times without having these seven questions in mind. I am noticing new details in the Gospel stories as I read with a different lens.

We saw how one sentence can pull out another facet for Gen Z in Mark 4:36: "There were also other boats with him." We were able to connect this with the question *Do all people matter to God?* Did God care about the people in those boats? What did they experience? Could they see or hear Jesus from where they were in the noise of a storm? Did they simply know they were in a storm that suddenly went quiet? What questions did they ask about God in those moments? Now, when I share with Gen Z about Jesus calming the storm in Mark 4:35-41, I say:

Maybe you have a difficult time believing God is real or thinking you have never experienced God's love or care in your life. Maybe you think God only cares about some people, like the disciples in the story. But there were other boats full of people on the water who also were caught in the storm and experienced the sudden calm. They would not have been able to see or hear Jesus from where they were, especially over the wind and waves.

What if you or others you care about were like the people in the other boats in this story? You just saw that you were in a storm, and it stopped, but you couldn't see or hear Jesus from the noise and chaos around you. What if it was indeed God who was in the storm with you and ceased the storm, and you just didn't realize it?

I had never seen this before I started paying attention to the questions Gen Z is asking, and I am experiencing the richness of Scripture in a new way through this process.

When I read about Jesus feeding the five thousand (John 6:1-14), I see touchpoints to the questions *Am I enough? Do all people matter to God? Can I trust you? Am I safe?* and fill out my worksheet (see table 2).

Table 2. My worksheet filled out for John 6:1-14

Gen Z Values	Which question does this passage address?	What is the response of the good news?
Is God good?		
Am I enough?	✔	What we have is enough for Jesus to do amazing feats! We simply give Jesus what we have. Jesus did not send the disciples to get more, but Andrew saw what they had.
Will you accept me?		

Gen Z Values	Which question does this passage address?	What is the response or the good news?
Do all people matter to God?	✔	Yes, Jesus cared about feeding all the people. He even facilitated feeding through a small boy, who some may have seen as an unlikely source!
Can I trust you?	✔	Yes, Jesus took everything the boy had, his whole lunch, and multiplied it so everyone ate, including the boy.
What is true?		
Am I safe?	✔	Yes, Andrew presented a solution but was also filled with doubt, asking, "How far will they go among so many?" Jesus did not reject the boy or rebuke Andrew but honored them by feeding all the people.

By using this format, I can lay out the possible directions to go with a given biblical passage. Often, time constraints for up-front speaking or Gen Z audience attention-span limitations prevent me from addressing all the questions a given passage may address. With the options spelled out side by side, I can consider which one or two questions I want to address, and go deeper with, as I share with my Gen Z audience.

In the working example of Jesus feeding the five thousand (John 6:1-14), I can now narrow my main point to share with my Gen Z audience:

It may feel risky to give God your whole life. I bet it felt risky for the little boy to give Jesus his whole lunch.

Maybe he wondered if he was going to have anything to eat after he gave his lunch up. What if Jesus takes the lunch, and the boy is left with nothing? That doesn't happen because that is not what God is like. We can see what God is like in this passage. The boy trusts God with his whole lunch, and God multiplies it. Not only does the boy get lunch, but God uses him to feed thousands of others. He uses what the boy has to care for thousands of others, feeding men, women, and children. We can trust him with our whole life. Can you imagine what God can do with the life you offer him?

As I go through the Bible with eyes for Gen Z, I see where their questions intersect with Scripture and the good news that is revealed.

FOR ALL PEOPLE EVERYWHERE

I have gained a deeper appreciation for God's Word in this process of contextualization. I appreciate that God's Word is for all people, everywhere, throughout history, because I am seeing the Bible engage with Gen Z's questions today. These are not the same questions I come to the Bible with. And yet, the Bible answers all of these questions. Isn't that incredible? I am seeing and experiencing the multifaceted nature of God's Word in real time, as new things come to light in familiar stories, passages, and Scriptures.

Let's walk through another example of how these questions can be overlaid in the reading, understanding, and teaching of Scripture in evangelism and discipleship. We are going to look at Romans 10:10-15 and identify where Gen Z's questions appear or are touched on in this passage.

For it is with your heart that you believe and are justified, and it is with your mouth that you profess your faith and are saved [*Am I enough? What is true? Can I trust you?*]. As Scripture says, "Anyone who believes in him will never be put to shame" [*Am I enough? Can I trust you? Do all people matter to God? Will you accept me? What is true? Am I safe?*]. For there is no difference between Jew and Gentile—the same Lord is Lord of all and richly blesses all who call on him [*Do all people matter to God? Is God good? Will you accept me?*], for, "Everyone who calls on the name of the Lord will be saved" [*Will you accept me? Is God Good? Am I enough? Can I trust you? Do all people matter to God? Am I safe?*].

How, then, can they call on the one they have not believed in? And how can they believe in the one of whom they have not heard? And how can they hear without someone preaching to them [*What is true? Is God good? Do all people matter to God?*]? And how can anyone preach unless they are sent? As it is written: "How beautiful are the feet of those who bring good news!" [*What is true? Do all people matter to God?*].

Notice how I read a very familiar passage slowly, keeping in mind the context of Gen Z's questions to see where the Bible intersects with them. While I do this, I work hard to put my own lens down, trying not to read and ask, "What does this mean to me?" but instead, "How does this meet Gen Z?" We uncover a powerful passage that answers Gen Z's questions, providing a direct connection between their values, experiences, and worldview and Scripture. Now, we have the opportunity to provide real responses from the Bible that are connected and relevant to their lives. It is an opportunity to demonstrate that the triune God is not irrelevant or out of touch, or just a concept floating around, but is personal and powerful.

As we read Romans 10:10-15, each of us may notice additional or different questions that these verses address. Go ahead and write them down on a notecard or in a journal. Like I said, Gen Z is asking more than seven questions, and we often know the Gen Zers in our life better than others do. What are they asking that this passage touches on?

I chose this passage because it reflects both evangelism and discipleship. It shares the gospel and explains how to become saved, and it also offers a charge to those who are disciples of Christ. In our evangelism, we learn to answer the questions our audience is asking with the good news of Jesus Christ. Now, let's look at Romans 10:10-15 one more time, this time paying attention to the features of a disciple:

> For it is with your heart that you believe and are justified, and it is with your mouth that you profess your faith and are saved [*Follower, Worshiper, Witness*]. As Scripture says, "Anyone who believes in him will never be put to shame" [*Follower, Prophet, Forgiver*]. For there is no difference between Jew and Gentile—the same Lord is Lord of all and richly blesses all who call on him [*Follower, Neighbor, Prophet*], for, "Everyone who calls on the name of the Lord will be saved" [*Follower*].
>
> How, then, can they call on the one they have not believed in? And how can they believe in the one of whom they have not heard? And how can they hear without

someone preaching to them [*Witness, Neighbor, Intercessor, Steward*]? And how can anyone preach unless they are sent? As it is written: "How beautiful are the feet of those who bring good news!" [*Witness, Prophet, Steward, Neighbor*].

Now we see the calling placed on the disciple's life. By going on this journey through God's Word together with Gen Z, engaging with how this passage answers their questions, we equip Gen Z to answer those questions for their peers. When we overlay the features of a disciple, we can now move from showing how the gospel responds to their questions to how they can live this out as a disciple. This passage becomes one that is a call to action out of remembering our identity in Christ: *Because you have these features of a disciple, go and live them out!*

Many of the features of a disciple I have connected with each verse are the corresponding feature to the question that verse addresses, but not all of them. Some of the features of a disciple listed next to each verse don't necessarily line up exactly with the questions asked. They don't match up every time.

Let's look at Romans 10:11, for example: "Anyone who believes in him will never be put to shame." This answers a lot of questions—*Am I enough? Can I trust you? Will you accept me? What is true? Am I safe? Do all people matter to God?*—but the features of a disciple I listed next to this verse are Follower, Forgiver, and Prophet.

- Follower: This verse connects with the Follower because those who "believe in him" are followers of Jesus Christ. Because "anyone who believes" isn't put to shame by God, then a disciple as Follower also should not put "anyone who believes" to shame.

- Prophet: Prophet was included because of the words "will never be put to shame." The Prophet has the gift and responsibility to notice if there are systems or people breaking with this and shaming others.

- Forgiver: Romans 10:11 also reflects that the disciple is compelled to be a Forgiver as one who is not put to shame. If Christ offers a reception without shame for those who believe, disciples of Christ can model the same. We do so by offering forgiveness, not the shame that comes with judgment and condemnation. This could possibly be stretched to Neighbor, as the disciple is in community with "anyone who believes," especially if in conversation around outcast, oppressed, and rejected ones "who believe," and their place in the Christian community.

I did not pair Worshiper, Witness, or Intercessor with Romans 10:11, even though they are related to the questions addressed by the verse. Mostly, because there is not an obvious direct connection to these features of a disciple. Romans 10:11 is not a call to pray for others or a call to testify and share one's story. It could be connected with the feature of Worshiper, but the term *believe* would need to be more fully fleshed out so as to reflect the act of putting total reliance and trust in God. That is not far-fetched, but it does take a little more work to make the connection.

Just because Romans 10:11 addresses the question *Am I safe?* does not mean the verse explicitly calls one to be an Intercessor. Just because it answers the question *What is true?* doesn't mean it is a command to share our story as a Witness. Could an argument be made that these features of a disciple fit Romans 10:11? Possibly, but they don't have to. We are not tasked with applying this system of always tying the Gen Z question directly with its correlating feature of a disciple in all Scriptures.

Some of the features provide a Christ-centered and biblical way to live out the generational value expressed in their questions, and some require a movement from one worldview to another. In other words, the feature of the disciple could be a corrective to the viewpoint from which the question is asked. When we are engaging with Scripture with a lens for Gen Z, we will have to read a verse, passage, section, or book repeatedly. The questions and features of a disciple are often directly connected to each other in a particular Scripture, but not always. We may read once with the questions in mind—okay, maybe a few times because it takes practice to see what we haven't seen before—then put those questions down, pick up the features of a disciple, and read it again.

When we are faced with the hard work of evangelism and discipleship, we can prefer an easy formula that provides a plug-and-play answer, like a YouTube tutorial that provides the step-by-step instructions to get from point A to point B. The practice I am presenting takes more work than that. Cross-generational work requires engagement with the next generation, Scripture, and the Holy Spirit to see what truth will come to light. We are invited on a journey of discovery!

10

READY TO GET STARTED?

The process in this book can be replicated. We looked at a question Gen Z is asking and the context around that question. We sought to understand how and why that question is being asked. Once we understood the context of a question Gen Z is asking, we provided a response through gospel presentation or discipleship. Then, we paired a feature of a disciple with Gen Z's question, as either a biblical expression of the heart of their question or a discipleship shift to a biblical understanding of their question.

The seven questions discussed not only came from studying Gen Z and their values, worldview, and experiences, but also came from my personal experiences with Gen Z. We take everything we have learned and blend it with our experiences with our Gen Z friends. As we engage with sharing the good news of Jesus Christ with our Gen Z audience, and disciple them in Christ, let's repeat these three steps: (1) listen, (2) remind, and (3) show.

LISTEN, LISTEN, LISTEN

Any conversation around generations provides generalized, overarching information about a large group of people. It does not account for the nuances and differences that pop up due to geography, school, family, personality, and so on. The ideas discussed in this book may not be every Gen Zer's experience, though it is their generational context, which means they aren't unaffected by it. Generational study will look for what people generally have in common with each other within an identified set of years. Generations are also made of individuals, each with a unique personality and set of experiences.

That's a lot of individuals we are talking about, individuals we know and spend time with, individuals we are ministering to. We have to do our homework on our Gen Z audience and on the Gen Zers in our lives. Throughout our process in this book, I peppered in some questions I like to ask Gen Zers in my life. If we are looking for a place to start, why not start with those:

- Introduction: Will you read this book with me?
- Chapter 1: What have you heard about your generation from older generations or the media?
- Chapter 2: What are some questions your friends or other people your age are asking about God? Do you think God is good? How do you define what is good?
- Chapter 3: How do you define what being "enough" means? What does it look like to forgive someone?
- Chapter 4: What does it look like to be accepted? Where have you seen people put God's Law in front of being a Neighbor? What would it be like if you realized how much God loved you? What prevents you from experiencing that?
- Chapter 5: Does God care about social justice? What do you notice? What do you have? What can you do with what you notice and what you have?

- Chapter 6: How do you know if you can trust someone?
- Chapter 7: How do you know something is true? Do you think you are free?
- Chapter 8: What kind of environment or person makes you feel safe?

Let's find time to get together with a Gen Zer in our lives to ask the questions above. We must pay attention to our experiences and conversations with Gen Z. Identify the questions each of our audiences are asking specifically. We can do so by asking additional questions, like:

- What are you celebrating?
- What are you worried about?
- What do you spend a lot of time thinking about?
- What do your friends spend a lot of time talking about?

Ask questions around God, faith, identity, purpose, community, or hope.[1] This is not a comprehensive list of questions or topics to discuss, but they will get the ball rolling. Listen and look for repeated themes. It is around those themes we can begin to identify the key questions our Gen Z friends are asking.

I was at a coffee shop with a couple Gen Z young women. They were complaining about social media, how it wastes their time, and how everything is so fake. Funnily enough, they were discussing this while scrolling social media. I put my hand on the table and leaned in to try to get their attention and said, "Can I ask you a question?" They both looked up, intrigued by my request. I continued, "What do you think people are looking for on social media? Why do you think they stay on it?"

They started listing things immediately: relationships, security, identity, affirmation, attention, and more. As we consider the responses by these young women, can we identify the questions they or their peers are asking when they get on social media? If they are looking for relationships or affirmation, they may be asking, "Will you like me?" (*Am I enough?*). If they are looking for identity, they may be asking, "Who am I?" If they are looking for security, they may be asking, "Will you stick around?" (*Can I trust you?*). We have to become astute listeners, listening for the questions behind what our Gen Z friends are sharing with us, and even listening for how they are finding those answers.

DON'T RUN FROM LAVA

Have we ever felt pushed away by a Gen Zer in our life, or experienced our loving, kind pursuit of them being met with spewing, volatile anger? Not all of our attempts to build relationships with our Gen Z friends are met with warmth and openness. Sometimes it can feel easier to throw our hands up and walk away than risk getting burned. We may even say to ourselves, *They know I'm there*, and then retreat and wait for that person to pursue us. I have to remind myself that it is not the younger person's job to pursue me; it is almost always my job to pursue them. In this way, I can demonstrate that I am indeed there.

What we really observed in that angry moment is that there is pain or tension from any number of sources residing under the surface. There was a flow of hot lava coursing through our Gen Z friend before we even arrived at the conversation, a cumulation of unanswered questions and unreconciled pain. This is a form of lament with nowhere to express it, so it ends up exploding on us sometimes. We see the heated tone, but we miss the longing, hopelessness, heartache, or suffering that created the tone in the first place. Let's not let the heated tone scare us away. Don't run away, lean in.

A couple years ago, I suffered a running injury that left me in chronic pain and unable to run. My nervous system was on fire all of the time, and any patience, tact, or flexibility I once possessed had gone out the window. My family and co-workers began to walk on eggshells around me so as not to set off another eruption. I was agitated by constant pain that consumed any physical, mental, or emotional energy, leaving no margin. Agitation, frustration, and anger came out of my pain, pain that had no simple or easy solution. I have to wonder, is this where Gen Z exists as they carry their anxiety, depression, loneliness, and hopelessness?

It is easy to retreat and back away from the volcano, but we are to approach and understand. We have to be the resilient ones. We have to keep showing up and we have to keep listening.

REMIND THEM WHO THEY ARE

Reminding Gen Z of who they are is part of both evangelism and discipleship. In evangelism, we reveal to Gen Z how God sees them and feels about them as it is revealed in Scripture. The enemy is working to kill, steal, and destroy Gen Z's identity. We fight back. We fight for the generations we are charged to care for, and we fight to remind Gen Z that they are God's beloved ones, who were always enough for him to make a way for them to know his love.

The enemy focuses his attack on those he fears, and I think there is something about Gen Z that scares the enemy. If this generation really understands who God is and who they are in Christ, they will be a global force of faith to reckon with.

For a generation who gives weight to accomplishments and failures as part of identity formation, it is important to remind Gen Z–aged disciples of Christ who they are. Too many times, I hear Gen Zers sheepishly confess how they should read their Bibles more or pray more. They list all the areas they are falling short in the Christian life and boil the life of a disciple down to the tasks they accomplish. The thinking behind this is, *If I do these things, then I am a Follower of God. If I don't do these things, then I guess I'm not.* Accomplishments determine Gen Z's sense of identity as Christ-following disciples.

Let's flip that around for our Gen Z audience. I want Gen Z to understand this: *Because I am a Follower of God, I do these things. They flow out of my identity as a disciple of Christ.* Their accomplishments don't determine their identity as a Follower of God, but being a Follower of God influences their actions. Part of this means that we, as mentors, pastors, practitioners, and parents, have to proactively and intentionally remind our Gen Z friends of who they are in Christ. Remind those Followers that they are also Forgivers, Worshipers, Witnesses, Neighbors, Stewards, Prophets, and Intercessors.

We have to find and create opportunities to do so with them, and not wait for moments that we hope will come up. This requires us to lean into being Intercessors (so we have direction from the Holy Spirit in what, how, and when to speak) and Neighbors (paying attention to and caring for our Gen Z community members).

SHOW AND TELL

Show Gen Z how the Bible answers real-world questions in evangelism and discipleship. We can even present a question, look at a passage of Scripture, and ask our Gen Z audience how they see God answering that question in the passage. Show them how the Bible is relevant, applicable, and practical to everyday life.

Gen Z, as well as the following generation (Gen Alpha), is a visual generation. They do not simply learn by listening to someone tell them something. They need to see it, and even better, they need to experience it. This means taking the unseen practices and experiences of a disciple and figuring out a way to make them seen and experienced. When we talk about submitting our will to God's will, let's find a way show it. When we worship, let's worship in a way that exhibits a position of total trust and reliance on God as Worshiper. When we take a walk outside, let's acknowledge God as Creator out loud and take a moment to notice his creation.

Will it feel forced and uncomfortable for us as we lean into this? Yes! But just because it's uncomfortable doesn't mean we shouldn't do it. We have an incredible opportunity to learn a new facet of what it means to be a disciple of Christ as we disciple others. It is time to try a new way to pass down the faith that we have —because whatever we are doing now is generally not working.

This extends to showing and telling how following Christ impacts the real world. So much of the conversation around spiritual things remains in the spiritual world, focused on internal personal decisions and spiritual commitments. It is imperative that older generations connect spiritual life with everyday life and its effect on community. After all, our physical bodies are where we engage our spiritual lives, and our communities are where we live out our faith. When I fast, or pray, or even work through forgiveness, I do so in this body. My breathing, heart rate, and tension or relaxation in my shoulders may be part of reflecting my spiritual engagement. It is only in community I can live out my identity as a Follower of God and practice forgiveness, witnessing, caring for others, and more.

Following the triune God through the saving work of Jesus Christ guided by the Holy Spirit should change everything, and I mean everything. From the moment I wake up, until I go to sleep, living as a disciple should impact every big and little, external and internal moment of my day.

Try this as an experiment: Take one day, and from the moment you wake up, jot down how being a Follower of God influences what you do. This can even include the time you wake: *I wake up early to go for a run to take care of the body God gave me, as a temple of the Holy Spirit, and because when I care for my physical health, I feel grateful for the body God has given me.* Notice how being a Follower of God has changed your habits, even if that habit started twenty years ago. Pay attention to how you spend money, drive your car, or deal with minor inconveniences. Log everything. We are not sharing with Gen Z an irrelevant faith in a disengaged and reckless God. Our faith changes everything, and we have to see it and recognize it in order to verbalize and demonstrate it.

As we share the gospel with Gen Z and disciple them, we may also have to remind ourselves that as Followers of God, we are also Forgivers, Worshipers, Witnesses, Neighbors, Stewards, Prophets, and Intercessors. We are not living an only-vertical relationship with God, but living horizontally to reflect the kingdom of heaven here on earth. Our faith isn't only about praying, reading the Bible, and going to church, but also about changing the communities we live in.

Gen Z is changing the world as we know it. Imagine Gen Z captivated by the love of God, living as disciples who are Followers of God, Forgivers, Worshipers, Witnesses, Neighbors, Stewards, Prophets, and Intercessors. Imagine the true freedom they will experience and bring to others as they live into that identity. This generation is globally connected and can create a movement in an instant. Let's do everything we can to set up this generation to know the saving life of Jesus Christ so they can be a force for the gospel across the world and for generations to come.

ACKNOWLEDGMENTS

I want to acknowledge the guidance, encouragement, and support from Dr. Peter Gurry, Dr. Arthur Satterwhite, Dr. Kim Nollan, Dr. Sean McGever, and Dr. Chap Clark. They helped me navigate what life and study look like after graduation and figure out how to steward years of education and research applied in the real world. This project is a direct outcome of their help. They will all say they did very little, but it is a good reminder that someone's small encouragement is a big deal to others.

I want to acknowledge my friends and colaborers in Young Life, who have shared their encouragement, insight, and experience with me throughout this project.

Thank you to my editor, Kelli Trujillo, who asked great questions, gave good encouragement, and walked with me at every step. Thank you to the whole team at InterVarsity Press for believing in this project.

Thank you to my husband and children, who were patient with me in the process and gave me the space to write (even if it was at five in the morning on most days).

A special thank you goes out to my Gen Z friends, who sat with me on my couch, at my kitchen counter, in my car, at coffee shops, and on buses to camp, who played with my children, and who shared their lives with me.

NOTES

INTRODUCTION

[1]The mission of Young Life is introducing adolescents to Jesus Christ and helping them grow in their faith.

[2]Tanita Maddox, "Gen Z as the Areopagus: Gospel Contextualization for a Generation" (DMin thesis, Phoenix Seminary, 2020).

[3]Jean M. Twenge, *iGen: Why Today's Super-Connected Kids Are Growing Up Less Rebellious, More Tolerant, Less Happy—and Completely Unprepared for Adulthood (and What This Means for the Rest of Us)* (New York: Simon and Schuster, 2018), 121.

[4]Aaron Earls, "Most Teenagers Drop Out of Church When They Become Young Adults," Lifeway Research, January 15, 2019, https://research.lifeway.com/2019/01/15/most-teenagers-drop-out-of-church-as-young-adults.

[5]Springtide Research Institute, "The State of Religion and Young People 2023: Exploring the Sacred" (Winona, MN: Springtide Research Institute, 2023), 16

[6]"Generation Z and the Future of Faith in America," *The Survey Center on American Life* (blog), accessed March 23, 2024, www.americansurveycenter.org/research/generation-z-future-of-faith.

[7]Mike Nappa, *The Jesus Survey: What Christian Teens Really Believe and Why* (Grand Rapids, MI: Baker Books, 2012).

[8]Springtide Research Institute, "The State of Religion and Young People 2023: Exploring the Sacred."

[9]"State of the Bible USA 2023" (American Bible Society, 2023), 97-98,https://1s712.americanbible.org/state-of-the-bible/stateofthebible/State_of_the_bible-2023.pdf; Paulus Widjaja, "Teaching Christian Character and Ethics to Generation Z," *The Conrad Grebel Review* 35, no. 1 (2017): 78.

[10]Springtide Research Institute, "The State of Religion and Young People 2023: Exploring the Sacred," 15.

[11]Pew Research Center, "1. How U.S. Religious Composition Has Changed in Recent Decades," Pew Research Center's Religion & Public Life Project, September 13, 2022, www.pewresearch.org/religion/2022/09/13/how-u-s -religious-composition-has-changed-in-recent-decades.

[12]Barna Group, *Gen Z: The Culture, Beliefs and Motivations Shaping the Next Generation* (Ventura, CA: Barna Group, 2018), 32.

[13]Reese Carlson, *Church Doesn't End With Z: Why Gen Z Is Leaving the Church and How to Reach Them* (pub. by author, 2022), 31-32.

[14]Kara Powell and Brad M. Griffin, *3 Big Questions That Change Every Teenager: Making the Most of Your Conversations and Connections* (Grand Rapids, MI: Baker Books, 2021), 33.

[15]Eric L. Mathis, *Worship with Teenagers: Adolescent Spirituality and Congregational Practice* (Grand Rapids, MI: Baker Academic, 2022), 112.

[16]Twenge, *iGen*; David Kinnaman, *unChristian: What a New Generation Really Thinks about Christianity and Why It Matters* (Grand Rapids, MI: Baker Books, 2007); James White, *Meet Generation Z: Understanding and Reaching the New Post-Christian World* (Grand Rapids, MI: Baker Books, 2017); Barna Group, *Gen Z*; Paul M. Gould, *Cultural Apologetics: Renewing the Christian Voice, Conscience, and Imagination in a Disenchanted World* (Grand Rapids, MI: Zondervan, 2019); Roberta Katz et al., *Gen Z, Explained: The Art of Living in a Digital Age* (Chicago: The University of Chicago Press, 2021).

[17]Powell and Griffin, *3 Big Questions That Change Every Teenager*, 31.

[18]Lesslie Newbigin, *Foolishness to the Greeks: The Gospel and Western Culture* (Grand Rapids, MI: Eerdmans, 1986), 134.

[19]Carlson, *Church Doesn't End With Z*, 168.

[20]If you are Gen Z, please send me your feedback! I like to say I study Gen Z, but Gen Z lives it. Help me understand your generation better by sharing with me your input and thoughts. They are so valuable!

I. WHO IS GENERATION Z?

[1]There is ongoing debate regarding the exact years Generation Z was born, and this range of birth years is an acceptable range. Many

estimations of the start of Gen Z include varying years in the mid-to-late nineties. The end of Gen Z and beginning of Gen Alpha is also the source of much debate. Jonathan Haidt, author of *The Anxious Generation*, speculates we will not see an end to Gen Z until our relationship with technology changes, and I'm inclined to agree. I also recognize a "cusp" or "micro-" generation: those born between 1994–1998 are Zillennials, who do not firmly fall into the generational descriptions and experiences of either the Millennial or Gen Z generations. Because they share some characteristics and experiences as Gen Z, they can often be included in conversations regarding the next generation.

[2]"20+ Gen Z Statistics For Employers in 2024—Hiring Guide," Qureos Hiring Guide, August 28, 2024, www.qureos.com/hiring-guide /gen-z-statistics.

[3]James White, *Meet Generation Z: Understanding and Reaching the New Post-Christian World* (Grand Rapids, MI: Baker Books, 2017), 49.

[4]Jean M. Twenge, *iGen: Why Today's Super-Connected Kids Are Growing Up Less Rebellious, More Tolerant, Less Happy—and Completely Unprepared for Adulthood (and What This Means for the Rest of Us)* (New York: Simon and Schuster, 2018), 49.

[5]Cassandra, "The Gen Z Effect," Cassandra, accessed March 28, 2020, https://cassandra.co/2017/the-gen-z-effect/gen-z-effect.

[6]Twenge, *iGen*, 55.

[7]Studies conducted by the National Survey of Drug Use and Health, Monitoring the Future, Pew Research Center, Bureau of Labor Statistics, and Centers for Disease Control and Prevention are summarized well by Dr. Jean Twenge in her book, *Generations: The Real Differences Between Gen Z, Millennials, Gen X, Boomers, and Silents—and What They Mean for America's Future* (New York: Atria Books, 2023).

[8]Mark E. Czeisler et al., "Mental Health, Substance Use, and Suicidal Ideation During the COVID-19 Pandemic—United States, June 24–30, 2020," *Morbidity Mortality Weekly Report* 2020, no. 69: 1049-57.

[9]Sally C. Curtin and Matthew F. Garnett, "Suicide and Homicide Death Rates Among Youth and Young Adults Aged 10–24: United States, 2001–2021," June 12, 2023, https://doi.org/10.15620/cdc:128423.

[10]US Department of Health and Human Services, "HHS, SAMHSA Release 2022 National Survey on Drug Use and Health Data," November 13, 2023, www.hhs.gov/about/news/2023/11/13/hhs-samhsa -release-2022-national-survey-drug-use-health-data.html.

[11]Springtide Research Institute, "The State of Religion and Young People: Mental Health: What Faith Leaders Need to Know" (Winona, MN: Springtide Research Institute, 2022), 11.

[12]Cigna, "New Cigna Study Reveals Loneliness at Epidemic Levels in America," *PR Newswire*, May 1, 2018, www.prnewswire.com/news -releases/new-cigna-study-reveals-loneliness-at-epidemic-levels-in -america-300639747.html.

[13]Jean M. Twenge et al., "Worldwide Increases in Adolescent Loneliness," *Journal of Adolescence* 93 (December 1, 2021): 266, https://doi .org/10.1016/j.adolescence.2021.06.006.

[14]Jean M. Twenge, "Increases in Depression, Self-Harm, and Suicide Among U.S. Adolescents After 2012 and Links to Technology Use: Possible Mechanisms," *Psychiatric Research and Clinical Practice* 2, no. 1 (2020): 19-25, https://doi.org/10.1176/appi.prcp.20190015.

[15]Jean M. Twenge, *Generations: The Real Differences Between Gen Z, Millennials, Gen X, Boomers, and Silents—and What They Mean for America's Future* (New York: Atria Books, 2023), 6-8.

[16]These questions are identified in my doctoral thesis, Tanita Maddox "Gen Z as the Areopagus: Gospel Contextualization for a Generation" (DMin thesis, Phoenix Seminary, 2020).

[17]Kathleen A. Cahalan, *Introducing the Practice of Ministry* (Collegeville, MN: Liturgical Press, 2010), 1–22, 128.

2. IS GOD GOOD?

[1]The Gen Z young professional was willing to do a phone call or meet in person, but the timing made a text conversation a good route. The amazing part was his willingness to discuss this topic over text messages. Sometimes I think older generations hesitate to ask big questions over text or in a direct message because we don't think it is appropriate or comfortable. In reality, our Gen Zers are comfortable with that format, and we could miss out on good conversations if we avoid texting.

[2]Almeda M. Wright, *The Spiritual Lives of Young African Americans* (New York: Oxford University Press, 2017), 71.

[3]Paul M. Gould, *Cultural Apologetics: Renewing the Christian Voice, Conscience, and Imagination in a Disenchanted World* (Grand Rapids, MI: Zondervan, 2019), 55.

[4]Springtide Research Institute, "The State of Religion and Young People 2023: Exploring the Sacred" (Winona, MN: Springtide Research Institute, 2023).

[5]Henri Nouwen further explores this topic in his book *Life of the Beloved* (1992).

[6]Emily Weinstein and Carrie James, *Behind Their Screens: What Teens Are Facing (and Adults Are Missing)* (Cambridge, MA: MIT Press, 2022), 124.

[7]For those who doubt whether the mental health crises, experiences, or diagnoses are real or blown out of proportion, Dr. Jean Twenge does a wonderful job in her book *Generations*, explaining how this kind of research is conducted, answering the objections to the reality of the increase in mental health issues, proving this is not just a subjective phenomenon, but a documented trend over decades. See Jean M. Twenge, *Generations: The Real Differences Between Gen Z, Millennials, Gen X, Boomers, and Silents—and What They Mean for America's Future* (New York: Atria Books, 2023).

[8]Springtide Research Institute, "The State of Religion and Young People: Mental Health: What Faith Leaders Need to Know" (Winona, MN: Springtide Research Institute, 2022), 11.

[9]Twenge, *Generations*, 394-411.

[10]"Key Substance Use and Mental Health Indicators in the United States: Results from the 2019 National Survey on Drug Use and Health," Substance Abuse and Mental Health Services Administration (SAMHSA), U.S. Department of Health and Human Services, accessed April 30, 2025.

[11]Twenge, *Generations*, 411.

[12]Marlies Maes et al., "Loneliness and Social Anxiety Across Childhood and Adolescence: Multilevel Meta-Analyses of Cross-Sectional and Longitudinal Associations," *Developmental Psychology* 55, no. 7 (2019): 1548-65, https://doi.org/10.1037/dev0000719.

[13]Ellie Polack, "New Cigna Study Reveals Loneliness at Epidemic Levels in America," Cigna Newsroom, May 1, 2018.

[14]Cigna Group, "The Cigna Group Newsroom—Vitality in America 2023," news release, accessed April 27, 2024, https://newsroom .thecignagroup.com/state-of-vitality-gen-z.

[15]Office of the Assistant Secretary for Health (OASH), "New Surgeon General Advisory Raises Alarm About the Devastating Impact of the Epidemic of Loneliness and Isolation in the United States," news release, May 3, 2023, www.hhs.gov/about/news/2023/05/03/new -surgeon-general-advisory-raises-alarm-about-devastating-impact -epidemic-loneliness-isolation-united-states.html.

[16]Jean M. Twenge et al., "Worldwide Increases in Adolescent Lone-liness," *Journal of Adolescence* 93 (December 1, 2021): 266, https://doi .org/10.1016/j.adolescence.2021.06.006.

[17]Springtide Research Institute, "The State of Religion and Young People: Mental Health," 39.

3. AM I ENOUGH?

[1]Young Life, "Relate: Knowing and Believing in the Next Generation" (2024), 17, 40, relate.younglife.org.

[2]Association for Psychological Science, "Social Media 'Likes' Impact Teens' Brains and Behavior," May 31, 2016, www.psychologicalscience.org/news /releases/social-media-likes-impact-teens-brains-and-behavior.html.

[3]CBS Reports, "Are the Kids All Right? The Internet," May 5, 2022, www .cbsnews.com/video/are-the-kids-all-right-the-internet-cbs-reports/.

[4]Kara Powell and Brad M. Griffin, *3 Big Questions That Change Every Teenager: Making the Most of Your Conversations and Connections* (Grand Rapids, MI: Baker Books, 2021), 97.

[5]Roberta Katz et al., *Gen Z, Explained: The Art of Living in a Digital Age* (Chicago: The University of Chicago Press, 2021), 43.

[6]Conflict and conflict resolution has not been modeled well for Gen Z. This is discussed around the question *Will you accept me?* Without op-tions of how to navigate disagreement or conflict, the option to simply walk away and dispose of the relationship becomes a viable option.

[7]Henri Nouwen, *Life of the Beloved* (New York: Crossroad Publishing Company, 1992), 31.

[8]Nouwen, *Life of the Beloved*, 129.

[9]Powell and Griffin, *3 Big Questions*, 115-21.

4. WILL YOU ACCEPT ME?

[1]Mora A. Reinka, Stephenie R. Chaudoir, and Diane M. Quinn, "Millennials Versus Gen Z: Have Perceptions and Outcomes of Concealable Stigmatized Identities Changed over Time?" *Stigma and Health*, February 15, 2024, https://doi.org/10.1037/sah0000515.

[2]"The Porn Phenomenon," Barna Group, accessed October 6, 2024, www.barna.com/the-porn-phenomenon/.

[3]Kara Powell and Brad M. Griffin, *3 Big Questions That Change Every Teenager: Making the Most of Your Conversations and Connections* (Grand Rapids, MI: Baker Books, 2021)

[4]Translation: I really hope you are enjoying this book so far. Some older generations think Gen Z is overemotional, entitled, fragile, and "too much," full of strangers to us, who need to get off their phones and get outside once in a while, but they are amazing. We, the older generations, are the ones who need to get out of our own mindset, lean in and understand, so we can understand why Gen Z is turned off by the Christian faith.

[5]Cambridge Dictionary Online, "Tolerance," accessed October 16, 2024, https://dictionary.cambridge.org/us/dictionary/english/tolerance.

[6]Melanie Curtin, "3 Ways Millennials Differ from Generation Z in 2019 Trends," Inc.com, January 29, 2019, www.inc.com/melanie-curtin/3-ways-millennials-differ-from-generation-z-in-2019-trends.html.

[7]Kara Powell and Brad M. Griffin present questions adolescents are facing in their development. Those questions are: Who am I? Where do I fit? What difference can I make? See Powell and Griffin, *3 Big Questions*.

[8]Andrew Root, *The End of Youth Ministry? Why Parents Don't Really Care About Youth Groups and What Youth Workers Should Do About It* (Grand Rapids, MI: Baker Academic, 2020), 88-90.

[9]Axis, "Dr. Carl Trueman On Gender, Identity, And Politics," *The Culture Translator* (podcast), August 21, 2024, https://axis.org/resource/the-culture-translator-podcast/dr-carl-trueman-on-gender-identity-and-politics/.

[10]Jean M. Twenge, *Generations: The Real Differences Between Gen Z, Millennials, Gen X, Boomers, and Silents—and What They Mean for America's Future* (New York: Atria Books, 2023), 362.

[11]Root, *The End of Youth Ministry?*, 56.

5. DO ALL PEOPLE MATTER TO GOD?

[1]By the early evening on the east coast, which was the afternoon on the west coast, CNN posted an article by AJ Willingham titled, "Blackout Tuesday: Why Posting a Black Image with 'Black Lives Matter' Hashtag Could Be Doing More Harm Than Good," June 2, 2020, www.cnn .com/2020/06/02/us/blackout-tuesday-black-lives-matter-instagram -trnd/index.html. Additional publications such as CBS News, *Variety*, *The Guardian*, *The Washington Post*, *Forbes*, and others also posted articles on June 2, 2020, sharing similar themes.

[2]In an article with NBC News, an author reflected on her own participation, referring to herself and others that posted a black square as "wannabe allies" who practiced "misguided, and frankly, lazy" allyship. Noor Noman, "'Blackout Tuesday' on Instagram Was a Teachable Moment for Allies like Me," June 6, 2020, www.nbcnews.com/think /opinion/blackout-tuesday-instagram-was-teachable-moment-allies -me-ncna1225961.

[3]These questions were discussed at Jude 3 Project's 2022 Courageous Conversations event. The Jude 3 Project is an incredible resource for pastors, ministers, and youth workers who are dealing with these kinds of questions in their community, and for anyone curious about the answers. I recommend checking out their content at jude3project .org.

[4]Almeda M. Wright, *The Spiritual Lives of Young African Americans* (New York: Oxford University Press, 2017), 63.

[5]Charles E. Goodman Jr., "Have We Lost the 'Soul' of the Black Church: Returning to Our Roots," *Theology Today* 81, no. 1 (2024): 40-49, https:// doi.org/10.1177/00405736231226096.

[6]Goodman Jr., "Have We Lost the 'Soul' of the Black Church," 45.

[7]Kathleen A. Cahalan, *Introducing the Practice of Ministry* (Collegeville, MN: Liturgical Press, 2010), 17.

[8]Cahalan, *Introducing the Practice of Ministry*, 17.

[9]Mark L. Strauss, *Four Portraits, One Jesus: A Survey of Jesus and the Gospels* (Grand Rapids, MI: Zondervan, 2007), 260.

6. CAN I TRUST YOU?

[1]Jeremy Finch, "What Is Generation Z, And What Does It Want?," *Fast Company*, May 4, 2015, www.fastcompany.com/3045317 /what-is-generation-z-and-what-does-it-want/.

[2]SWNS, "Gen Zers Are Living a 'Double Life': Study," May 29, 2024, https://nypost.com/2024/05/29/lifestyle/gen-zers-are-living -a-double-life-study/.

[3]Tobias Faix, "Hybrid Identity: Youth in Digital Networks, A Model of Contextualization for Youth Ministry," *Journal of Youth and Theology* 15 (2016): 65-87; Barna Group, *Gen Z: The Culture, Beliefs and Motivations Shaping the Next Generation* (Ventura, CA: Barna Group, 2018), 32; Mission Hills Church, "Episode 3 | The Changes in the Next Gen w/ Dr. Chap Clark (PhD)," May 14, 2024, YouTube, www.youtube.com /watch?v=MMdgcsxkmP0.

[4]A simple search on the internet for "Teacher fired for OnlyFans" will produce a number of headlines.

[5]Stephanie Rivas-Lara et al., "Teens and Screens: Romance or Nomance," UCLA Center for Scholars and Storytellers, October 2024, 17, www .scholarsandstorytellers.com/css-teens-and-screens-2023-report.

[6]Roberta Katz et al., *Gen Z, Explained: The Art of Living in a Digital Age* (Chicago: The University of Chicago Press, 2021), 124.

[7]Young Life, "*YLTV Episode 5—YLTV Relates to Gen Z*," October 7, 2024, YouTube, www.youtube.com/watch?v=ccqF2le41f4.

[8]Springtide Research Institute, "The State of Religion and Young People 2023: Exploring the Sacred" (Winona, MN: Springtide Research Institute, 2023), 5.

[9]Eric L. Mathis, *Worship with Teenagers: Adolescent Spirituality and Congregational Practice* (Grand Rapids, MI: Baker Academic, 2022), 105.

[10]Kathleen A. Cahalan, Introducing the Practice of Ministry (Collegeville, MN: Liturgical Press, 2010), 8.

[11]Frederick Dale Bruner, *Matthew: A Commentary*, vol. 1: The Christbook, Matthew 1–12 (Grand Rapids, MI: Eerdmans, 2004), 123.

7. WHAT IS TRUE?

[1]Jude 3 Project, "What Is New Age Spirituality? | Signs of New Age Series Pt. 1," June 4, 2024, YouTube, www.youtube.com/watch?v=1RuUgDiaR5s; Jude 3 Project, "Why Do New Age Spiritual Practices Seem to Be Effective?

| Signs of New Age Series Pt. 2," June 12, 2024, www.youtube.com /watch?v=xMUeSOZJpsE.

[2]John Kim, "How to Find Your Truth," December 5, 2023, Psychology Today,www.psychologytoday.com/us/blog/the-angry-therapist/202312 /how-to-find-your-truth.

[3]Eric L. Mathis, *Worship with Teenagers: Adolescent Spirituality and Congregational Practice* (Grand Rapids, MI: Baker Academic, 2022), 90.

[4]"Let It Go" (performed by Idina Menzel), from the motion picture *Frozen*, music and lyrics by Kristen Anderson-Lopez and Robert Lopez, Walt Disney Animation Studios, 2013.

[5]Lene Jensen et al., "It's Wrong, But Everybody Does It: Academic Dishonesty Among High School and College Students," *Contemporary Educational Psychology* 27 (2002): 209-28, https://doi.org/10.1006 /ceps.2001.1088.

[6]Allyson Banks, "Millennials and Gen Z Lie in Their Resumes More than Boomers," Converus (blog), January 28, 2020, https://converus.com /blog/millenials-and-gen-z-lie-in-their-resumes-more-than -boomers/.

[7]Axis, "Dr. Carl Trueman On Gender, Identity, And Politics," The Culture Translator (podcast), August 21, 2024, https://axis.org /resource/the-culture-translator-podcast/dr-carl-trueman-on-gender -identity-and-politics/.

[8]Andrew Root, *The End of Youth Ministry? Why Parents Don't Really Care About Youth Groups and What Youth Workers Should Do About It* (Grand Rapids, MI: Baker Academic, 2020), 55.

[9]Kara Powell and Brad M. Griffin, *3 Big Questions That Change Every Teenager: Making the Most of Your Conversations and Connections* (Grand Rapids, MI: Baker Books, 2021), 93.

[10]Root, *The End of Youth Ministry?*, 138.

[11]Sally Lloyd-Jones, *The Jesus Storybook Bible* (Grand Rapids, MI: Zonderkidz, 2007), 272.

8. AM I SAFE?

[1]In her book *The Emotional Lives of Teenagers: Raising Connected, Capable and Compassionate Adolescents* (Great Britain: Atlantic Books, 2023), Lisa Damour discusses parents' uneasiness with emotional distress.

[2]Damour, *The Emotional Lives of Teenagers*, 17.

[3]Jonathan Haidt discusses the impact of this focus on safety at length on college campuses in *The Coddling of the American Mind* and for children and young people in *The Anxious Generation*.

[4]Jonathan Haidt, *The Anxious Generation: How the Great Rewiring of Childhood Is Causing an Epidemic of Mental Illness* (New York: Penguin Press, 2024), 88.

[5]Haidt, *The Anxious Generation*, 85-93.

[6]Jean M. Twenge, *iGen: Why Today's Super-Connected Kids Are Growing Up Less Rebellious, More Tolerant, Less Happy—and Completely Unprepared for Adulthood (and What This Means for the Rest of Us)* (New York: Simon and Schuster, 2018), 159.

[7]C. S. Lewis, *The Lion, the Witch and the Wardrobe* (Zondervan, 1994), 80.

10. READY TO GET STARTED?

[1]Kara Powell and Brad M. Griffin's book *3 Big Questions That Change Every Teenager: Making the Most of Your Conversations and Connections* (Grand Rapids, MI: Baker Books, 2021) is full of questions that are not limited to teenagers.

Like this book?

Scan the code to discover more content like this!

Get on IVP's email list to receive special offers, exclusive book news, and thoughtful content from your favorite authors on topics you care about.

ĩvp | InterVarsity Press

IVPRESS.COM/BOOK-QR